FIRST
FUN
ANIMAL
ENCYCLOPEDIA

First published in 2005 by Miles Kelly Publishing Ltd
Bardfield Centre, Great Bardfield, Essex CM7 4SL

2 4 6 8 10 9 7 5 3

This edition published in 2007

This title is also available in hardback

British Library Cataloguing-in-Publication Data
A catalogue record for this book is available from the British Library

ISBN 978-1-84236-614-1

Printed in China

Editorial Director
Belinda Gallagher

Art Director
Jo Brewer

Editors
Nicola Sail, Amanda Learmonth

Assistant Editor
Lucy Dowling

Designer
Debbie Meekcoms

Design Assistant
Maya Currell

Reprographics
Anthony Cambray, Liberty Newton, Ian Paulyn

Indexer
Jane Parker

Production Manager
Elizabeth Brunwin

www.mileskelly.net
info@mileskelly.net

FIRST FUN ANIMAL ENCYCLOPEDIA

Steve Parker

Miles Kelly

PUBLISHING

Contents

How to use this book

Your *First Fun Animal Encyclopedia* is bursting with information, colour pictures and fun activities. The pages run from A to Z with a new subject on every page. This will help you find information quickly and easily. There are cartoons to bring amazing true facts to life and puzzles and games to tease your brain. The index at the back of the book will help you look for specific information.

Colour bands
Your encyclopedia has six subject areas. The coloured bands along the top of each page tell you which subject area you are in.
- Birds has red bands.
- Mammals has orange bands.
- Insects and other invertebrates has green bands.
- Habitats has purple bands.
- Reptiles, amphibians and fish has blue bands.
- Behaviour, breeding and life cycle has yellow bands.

Pictures
Illustrations or photographs accompany each caption. Many illustrations are labelled to explain the different parts in more detail.

Alphabet strip
Your book is alphabetical. This means it runs from A to Z. Along the bottom of every page is an alphabet strip. The letter that starts the main heading is in bold. Above the letter there is a small arrow to highlight where you are in the alphabet.

Activity and puzzle boxes
Some pages will have activities, games or puzzles for you to do. Look for the green or blue panels.

Bears

Find out more:
Arctic animals ◄ Mammals ►

Bears are big, powerful mammals. They have a large head, wide body, massive legs, huge paws and claws and a tiny tail. Most live in forests and eat mainly plant foods. The biggest is the polar bear, which is white and eats meat, and the brown bear or grizzly.

▼ Sun bear
The sun bear lives in the trees of Southeast Asia. It stands about 1.4 metres tall and weighs around 50 kilograms, making it the smallest bear. Its tongue can stick out 25 centimetres to lick honey from bees' nests, grubs from wood holes and termites from their nests.

▲ Spectacled bear
The only bear of South America, the spectacled bear has pale eye rings and rarely leaves the trees of upland forests. It bends branches over to make a rough nest, to rest and sleep.

Bear senses
Do bears find their food and their way around using mainly their eyes, ears or nose? Put these bear senses in order, from the strongest to the weakest:

**ears and hearing
eyes and sight
nose and smell**

answers
1. nose and smell, 2. ears and hearing, 3. eyes and sight.

▼ Fishing for salmon
Like most bears, grizzlies eat many foods – roots, nuts, berries, grubs, birds' eggs, honey and occasionally meat. In autumn, grizzlies gather along rivers to catch salmon. A grizzly then sleeps for much of the winter in a cave or den.

Wow!
The grizzly bear is the largest land-based carnivore (meat-eater), standing 3 metres tall and weighing up to 1 tonne.

A-Z of bears
American black bear – middle of North America
Asiatic black bear – south and east Asia (mainland)
Brown bear (grizzly) – northern Europe, Asia and North America
Giant panda – west and south China
Polar bear – all around the Arctic
Sloth bear – southern Asia
Spectacled bear – uplands of western South America
Sun bear – Southeast Asia

18　a **b** c d e f g h i j k l m n o p q r s t u v w x y z

Main text
Every page begins with a paragraph introducing each subject.

Cross-references
Within the colour band are cross-references to other subjects. These tell you where you can find more information about your chosen topic. Follow the arrows to turn backwards or forwards to the correct page.

Beavers

Find out more:
Mice and rats ▶ Rodents ▶

Beavers are big, stocky members of the rat-and-mouse group – rodents. They gnaw strongly with their incisor teeth and eat bark, soft wood, sap, fruits and leaves. Biggest and most common of the three types is the American beaver. It has a wide, flat, scaly-looking tail and lives in family groups across North America, and also in parts of northern Europe and Asia.

▼ Beavers at work

The beaver family is busy all day. The beavers build a dam from branches, stones and mud, across a stream. This holds back the water to make a lake where the beavers live in their lodge. Beavers keep busy repairing their lodge and gathering food — mainly soft bark, shoots, buds and twigs.

▲ Mountain beaver

This secretive beaver has almost no tail and rarely swims. It looks like a big, fat rat and lives in a burrow in the woods along North America's west coast.

beavers gnaw around trunks to fell trees, using the branches to build a dam and lodge

Captions
Captions give you detailed information about all the photographs and illustrations in your book.

the lodge's living platform is dry and safe

Word box

incisor
a tooth with a straight, sharp edge, like a chisel or spade, at the front of the mouth

lodge
the den or 'house' of a beaver family

the lodge's underwater entrance and thick walls keep out enemies such as wolves

Wow!

When well-fed in autumn, the European beaver is the second-heaviest rodent weighing over 35 kilograms (the capybara is the heaviest at 66 kilograms).

underwater, a beaver sees well and feels with long whiskers

Wow boxes
Look for the orange panels to read amazing true facts — the funny cartoons will make you laugh!

a **b** c d e f g h i j k l m n o p q r s t u v w x y z **19**

Word boxes
New or difficult words are explained in the yellow panels.

Amphibians

Find out more:
Desert animals ▶ Fliers and gliders ▶ Frogs and toads ▶
Poisonous animals ▶ River and lake animals ▶

Most amphibians live in tropical rainforests and swamps. There are 5,000 different kinds. Salamanders and newts have four legs and a tail. Frogs and toads do not have a tail. Caecilians have neither a tail nor legs and look more like worms. Most amphibians start life in water as legless tadpoles or larvae, and gradually move onto land as they grow legs and become adults.

▶ Back to water

Most adult amphibians return to the water to breed. Some become very colourful to attract a mate. The male great crested newt develops a bright red underside and frilly back crest.

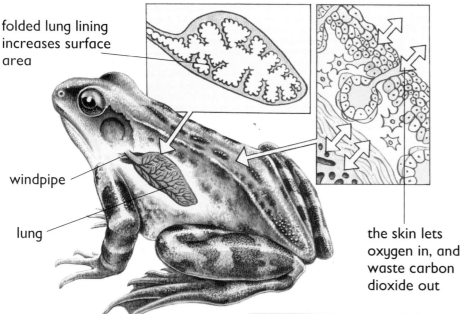

folded lung lining increases surface area

windpipe

lung

the skin lets oxygen in, and waste carbon dioxide out

▲ How amphibians breathe

Adult amphibians breathe air in and out of their lungs, like we do. But they also absorb (soak in) air through their damp skin. If the skin dries out, many types of amphibians die from suffocation.

Word box

amphibian
a cold-blooded animal that lives in water when young, and on land when grown-up

metamorphosis
when an animal grows and changes body shape

Wow!

The biggest amphibians are Asian giant salamanders, 1.7 metres long. The smallest are sminthillus frogs of Cuba — shorter than this word 'frog'.

▼ Green as the forest leaves

Many amphibians are coloured to blend in with their surroundings. This is called camouflage. The red-eyed tree frog matches green leaves, which it grips with its sucker-like toe tips.

▼ Growing up

Amphibians begin life as spotlike, jelly-covered eggs called spawn. These are laid in water or a damp place. They hatch into larvae (tadpoles), with feathery gills on their heads, which they use to breathe under water. This fire salamander larva is undergoing metamorphosis. It is growing legs and will soon move onto land.

Animal behaviour

Find out more:
Apes ▶ Birds ▶ Courtship ▶ Mammals ▶

Behaviour describes what an animal does – its actions and movements. Some animals, like worms and slugs, have very simple behaviour. A worm does little except try to avoid light, dryness and being touched, and will just eat its way through soil. Other animals, especially birds and mammals, have complicated behaviour.

▶ Clever behaviour?

Some animals can use tools. The Egyptian vulture picks up a stone in its beak to use as a hammer. It then smashes open an egg so it can eat what is inside. But if we replace the real egg by a painted wooden one, the vulture still keeps trying to smash it. So maybe this bird is not so clever after all! The cleverest birds are probably members of the parrot and crow families.

Wow!

Some gorillas 'talk' to the human guards who protect them from poachers (thieves), using the sign language they have invented themselves.

▼ Learned and not learned

An orb-web spider can make its intricate web without watching or learning from other spiders. Its behaviour is 'built in' from the start, rather than learned later. This is called instinct.

▼ Breeding behaviour

In the breeding season, male mammals like impalas, deer and goats clash heads and fight each other. This behaviour is called rutting. The strongest, healthiest male wins the contest and is able to mate with the females. This means his offspring are likely to be strong and healthy too.

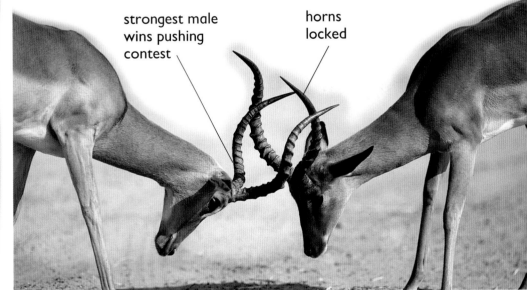

strongest male wins pushing contest

horns locked

Shape puzzle

Can you put these shapes in an order that makes sense? Some chimps can!

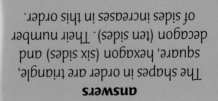

answers
The shapes in order are triangle, square, hexagon (six sides) and decagon (ten sides). Their number of sides increases in this order.

Animal societies

Find out more:
Insects ▶ Nests ▶ Wolves and dogs ▶

Most animals spend much of their lives alone.
But some live with others of their kind, usually sharing jobs such as cleaning and finding food, warning of danger and even protecting each other. These groups are called animal societies. It is mainly insects, birds and mammals that form these societies. Usually there is just one leader.

▶ One for all, all for one

Bees form a society together, as do wasps, ants and termites. Worker bees clean the nest, gather food and tend grubs (young). They communicate by touches, smells and movements called 'dances'. They attack and sting an enemy to protect their very close family.

▲ Sentry duty

Social living means there are many eyes and ears to detect danger. In southern African grasslands, some meerkats take turns to watch for danger while the others feed. When the lookout barks or growls, all the members race down into their burrows.

Word scramble

Unscramble these words to find the names of five animals that form societies:

a. TESTMERI
b. LASROGLI
c. NAST
d. WIERDBRAVES
e. SEVLOW

answers
a. termites b. gorillas c. ants d. weaverbirds e. wolves

▶ Bird 'skyscraper'

Sociable weaverbirds make a huge shared nest in an acacia tree. Each male and female has its own chamber, but the whole nest may contain over 200 birds. They are safe in numbers as they squawk, flap and peck enemies. They also feed together, always watching each other. If one finds food, the others gather to share it.

Antarctic animals

Find out more:
Arctic animals ▶ Migrating animals ▶
Seals and sea lions ▶

Antarctica is a huge frozen region at the South Pole. The cold Southern Ocean is rich in nutrients and plankton that are eaten by small fish, squid and krill. These then become food for larger fish, penguins, seabirds, seals and great whales.

Antartica

Word box

krill
small, shrimplike creatures of the ocean

plankton
tiny plants and animals drifting in water

◀ Cold fish

The cold Antarctic water is full of cod, sea perch, ice fish and tooth fish. They are prey for the Southern elephant seal, which can dive down to 400 metres.

▼ Antarctic predator

One of the biggest predators (hunters) in the Antarctic seas is the fierce, sharp-toothed leopard seal. It is more than 3 metres long and hunts penguins, seabirds, fish, squid and even small seals.

▼ A chilly wait

Penguins live in Antarctica. The female emperor penguin lays her egg and then goes off to feed at sea. The male stands with the egg on his feet all winter. He feeds the chick when it hatches with food stored in his stomach, until the female returns to take over.

▶ Summer visitors

Some animals journey to Antarctica only for the brief, warm summer. The Arctic tern migrates all the way from the Arctic, near the North Pole, to feed on small creatures at the water's surface. Whales migrate from warm, tropical regions to eat vast shoals of krill.

Wow!

The male Southern elephant seal is as big as a real elephant – almost 6 metres long and 5 tonnes in weight!

Anteaters and sloths

Find out more:
Insects ▶ Mammals ▶

three-toed sloth

Anteaters, sloths, armadillos and pangolins live slow, secretive lives.
They are mainly active at night, although sloths are hardly active at all! Anteaters and pangolins have no teeth and eat small insects. Sloths munch leaves, shoots and fruits. Armadillos eat many foods, and have small, weak molar teeth.

▶ Scaly ball

Pangolins live in Africa and Asia, both on the ground and in trees. Like an armadillo, a pangolin can curl into a ball, completely protected by its hard plates of bone and horn. It licks up insect food with a long, sticky, flicking-out tongue.

▶ Insect-eater

The giant anteater of South America rips open an ant nest or termite mound and licks up a few hundred insects with its very long tongue.

▲ Grub-digger

The armadillo shuffles about at night and digs for grubs, worms, termites, shoots and fruits. Its daytime den is a long, deep burrow. When in danger it rolls into a hard-cased ball.

◀ Slow descent

A sloth usually hangs upside down from a branch, gripping with its long claws. It only comes down if it cannot reach another tree through the branches. The sloth drags itself along the ground on bent knuckles, watching for predators such as jaguars.

Juicy 'ants'

Pretend that some raisins are ants. Put some on a plate and try eating them like an anteater, with your tongue – no fingers! An anteater can lick up more than 300 ants each minute. How many can you eat?

Antelopes and gazelles

Find out more:
Cattle ▶ Deer ▶ Mammals ▶

Antelopes are long-legged, fast-running, grazing animals that live in Africa and Asia. Gazelles are similar but slightly slimmer, smaller and speedier. Both are hoofed mammals, cousins of cows and goats. Most have long, curving horns, which are always growing slowly.

Wow!

An impala can jump more than 10 metres in one bound.

▼ Wild beast?

The wildebeest or gnu is a large antelope of African grasslands. Like most antelopes and gazelles, the females live in large herds. Males stay around the edge of the herd and form their own groups.

▼ Diving duiker

Duikers are small antelopes from central and southern Africa. Their name means 'divers' because they are very shy and dive into thick undergrowth to escape. Unusually for antelopes, they live alone or in pairs. They eat plants, termites, ants and even snakes!

▲ Ready to go

The springbok of southern Africa is a very fast gazelle, bounding at more than 50 kilometres an hour. Like many antelopes and gazelles, herds migrate with the seasons to find fresh grass and water.

▼ At the waterhole

Kudus live in woods and grassland. At waterholes around dawn and dusk, they use keen senses of sight, hearing and smell to detect danger. A calf can run from enemies less than one hour after birth.

Word scramble

Unscramble these words to find the names of four antelopes and gazelles:

a. SOMTHON'S LEZAGEL
b. ALAPIM
c. DELNA
d. OXYR

answers
a. thomson's gazelle b. impala
c. eland d. oryx

Apes

Our closest animal cousins are apes. Their body shape is similar to ours. They are clever and use tools, and most live in groups called troops. The smaller apes are gibbons of Southeast Asian rainforests. The larger apes are chimpanzees and gorillas, from Africa, and orang-utans, from Southeast Asia. All apes are rare and need our protection.

◀ Grooming friends

Chimps form large troops, of 100 members or more. Friends in a troop groom each other's fur and sleep in tree-nests at night. They eat plants, small animals and birds. Males can form a 'gang' to hunt monkeys or attack wandering chimps from other troops.

▲ The biggest ape

A full-grown male gorilla, or silverback, stands almost 2 metres tall and weighs over 200 kilograms. He defends his small troop of 5 to 15 against other gorillas and predators, such as leopards. But most of the time, gorillas just munch plants, sleep, groom or play.

Word box

territory
an area where an animal lives, feeds and defends itself or its group against other animals or danger

▶ The lonely ape

There are two kinds of orang-utans: Bornean and Sumatran. Unlike other apes, they live mainly alone, except for a mother and her baby. Like most apes, orang-utans are mostly vegetarian, eating fruits, shoots, buds, flowers and leaves. They rarely leave their trees.

▲ Noisy gibbons

Gibbons, such as the white-handed or lar gibbon, live in small family groups. They whoop and holler at dawn and dusk to defend their territory. They can make 10-metre swings through the treetops.

Arctic animals

Find out more:
Antarctic animals ◄
Bears ► Owls ► Whales ►

The Arctic Ocean, in the far north of the world, is almost totally covered in winter by a huge floating ice sheet. The land around is frozen, yet animals still thrive. Fish, seals and whales swim in open water. Polar bears, musk ox, Arctic foxes and hares roam the land. Snowy owls swoop around above the icy ground.

Word box

blubber
a fatty substance under the skin of mammals and birds, which keeps in warmth

tundra
treeless, boggy land around the Arctic Ocean covered in winter snow

bowhead whale

▲ Giants in the sea

Some great whales, like the 20-metre-long, 60-tonne bowhead, stay in Arctic waters all year. Others, such as blue and minke whales, arrive only for summer. Like seals, they have a thick layer of blubber to keep them warm.

▼ Adaptable bear

Polar bears eat meat, such as caribou, seals, birds, whales and fish. The female digs a snow den in early winter. Without eating any food, she stays here and gives birth to two or three cubs, feeding them on her milk.

▲ Musk ox

Large herds of musk oxen roam the tundra. Their long fur keeps out the cold. They scrape away snow with their large hooves to find plants to eat. If a predator appears, oxen stand in a circle, facing outwards, to protect their young in the middle.

◄ Winter white

Many Arctic animals, like snowy owls, are white in winter, to blend in with snow and ice. This camouflage makes them less noticeable to predators and prey.

Wow!

The bowhead whale has the largest mouth of any animal, almost 10 metres around the lips!

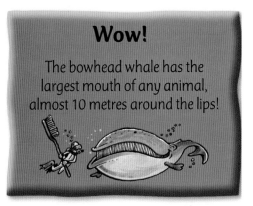

Baby animals

Find out more:
Birds ▶ Eggs ▶ Mammals ▶ Nests ▶ Reptiles ▶

Many kinds of baby animals survive without help from their parents. Insects, and most fish and amphibians, hatch from eggs and survive on their own. But some reptile parents, and almost all birds and mammals, care for their babies.

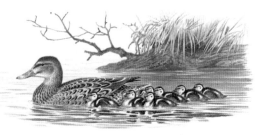

▲ Mother duck

After hatching, the mother cares for her ducklings, who follow her everywhere. Ducklings use sounds when in trouble, cheeping loudly if they are lost.

▼ Helpless baby

Like all baby mammals, the young baboon feeds on its mother's milk. It clings to its mother for warmth. As with most other large mammals, baboons usually have just one baby.

▲ Big baby

A young elephant is a 'baby' longer than almost any other animal. It feeds on its mother's milk for two years, and stays near her for another three. Many females in the herd help to protect the baby.

▼ Help with hatching

The female of nearly all crocodiles and alligators makes a caring mother. She guards her eggs and babies fiercely. The babies squeak loudly in their eggs. The mother helps them to hatch, carries them gently to a quiet pool, and guards them for several weeks.

American alligator

Baby quiz

What animal will each of these babies grow up to be?

1. foal **2.** cub
3. leveret **4.** calf **5.** kid

Choose from:
a. tiger **b.** goat
c. whale **d.** horse **e.** hare

answers
1d 2a 3e 4c 5b

Bats

Bats are the only mammals that can fly.
There are almost 1,000 kinds of bat (nearly one-fifth
of all mammals) and most live in tropical forests.
They are tiny, and flit about at night after flying insects.
Bigger, more powerful bats hunt fish, small birds
and owls. Most bats rest by day in dark,
sheltered places like caves, hollow trees
and the roofs of buildings.

flying foxes

high-pitched
sounds echo
off the moth

common
pipistrelle

▲ Squeaks in the night

Most bats find their way in the
dark helped by both eyes and ears.
Bats make high-pitched sounds
that bounce off nearby objects as
echoes. The bat hears the echoes
and can work out the position of
objects as small as a gnat.

Wow!
Bats have strong muscles to
power their wings. Some can fly
at more than 50 kilometres
an hour!

▲ Bat roosts

Bats usually rest or roost
by day in groups. They hang
upside down by their clawed feet,
wrapped up in their wings. The
wings are the bat's 'arms',
designed for flight. They are
made of a thin, light, tough
membrane, which is held out by
extremely long finger bones.

▶ Fruit bats

About 190 kinds of bats are fruit
bats, called 'flying foxes' due to their
long-snouted faces. They eat fruits,
seeds, shoots and plant juices but
can be pests and ruin farm crops.

Word box

echo
sound that has bounced, or has
been reflected, off an object

membrane
a thin layer of skinlike substance,
on or inside the body of an
animal or plant

Bears

Bears are big, powerful mammals. They have a large head, wide body, massive legs, huge paws and claws and a tiny tail. Most live in forests and eat mainly plant foods. The biggest is the polar bear, which is white and eats meat, and the brown bear or grizzly.

▼ Sun bear

The sun bear lives in the trees of Southeast Asia. It stands about 1.4 metres tall and weighs around 50 kilograms, making it the smallest bear. Its tongue can stick out 25 centimetres to lick honey from bees' nests, grubs from wood holes and termites from their nests.

▲ Spectacled bear

The only bear of South America, the spectacled bear has pale eye rings and rarely leaves the trees of upland forests. It bends branches over to make a rough nest, to rest and sleep.

Bear senses

Do bears find their food and their way around using mainly their eyes, ears or nose? Put these bear senses in order, from the strongest to the weakest:

**ears and hearing
eyes and sight
nose and smell**

answers
1. nose and smell, 2. ears and hearing, 3. eyes and sight.

▼ Fishing for salmon

Like most bears, grizzlies eat many foods – roots, nuts, berries, grubs, birds' eggs, honey and occasionally meat. In autumn, grizzlies gather along rivers to catch salmon. A grizzly then sleeps for much of the winter in a cave or den.

Wow!

The grizzly bear is the largest land-based carnivore (meat-eater), standing 3 metres tall and weighing up to 1 tonne.

A-Z of bears

American black bear – middle of North America
Asiatic black bear – south and east Asia (mainland)
Brown bear (grizzly) – northern Europe, Asia and North America
Giant panda – west and south China
Polar bear – all around the Arctic
Sloth bear – southern Asia
Spectacled bear – uplands of western South America
Sun bear – Southeast Asia

Beavers

Beavers are big, stocky members of the rat-and-mouse group – rodents. They gnaw strongly with their incisor teeth and eat bark, soft wood, sap, fruits and leaves. Biggest and most common of the three types is the American beaver. It has a wide, flat, scaly-looking tail and lives in family groups across North America, and also in parts of northern Europe and Asia.

▼ Beavers at work

The beaver family is busy all day. The beavers build a dam from branches, stones and mud, across a stream. This holds back the water to make a lake where the beavers live in their lodge. Beavers keep busy repairing their lodge and gathering food – mainly soft bark, shoots, buds and twigs.

▲ Mountain beaver

This secretive beaver has almost no tail and rarely swims. It looks like a big, fat rat and lives in a burrow in the woods along North America's west coast.

beavers gnaw around trunks to fell trees, using the branches to build a dam and lodge

the lodge's living platform is dry and safe

the lodge's underwater entrance and thick walls keep out enemies such as wolves

Word box

incisor
a tooth with a straight, sharp edge, like a chisel or spade, at the front of the mouth

lodge
the den or 'house' of a beaver family

underwater, a beaver sees well and feels with long whiskers

Wow!

When well-fed in autumn, the European beaver is the second-heaviest rodent weighing over 35 kilograms (the capybara is the heaviest at 66 kilograms).

Beetles

Beetles are the largest single animal group on Earth. There are more than 350,000 kinds. These insects live in every habitat, from icy mountains to deserts and deep lakes (but not the sea). A beetle has two hard, curved wing-cases over its body, which are really its toughened front pair of wings. Underneath, folded up, are the second pair of large flying wings.

▲ Lady beetle

A ladybird's colourful spots warn other animals: 'I taste horrible, don't touch me!'. They are a gardener's best friend. Ladybirds protect garden plants by eating huge numbers of caterpillars and aphids (greenfly and blackfly).

▼ Ferocious beetle

The male rhinoceros beetle is one of the longest in the world, at 18 centimetres. The male uses his huge head horn to fight off other males and attract the smaller-horned female for breeding.

▲ Beetle lookalike

Cockroaches have a tough body covering and look similar to beetles. But they belong to a different insect group (*Blattodea*). Most kinds live in tropical forests. A few invade buildings, coming out at night to eat scraps of food.

▶ Great diving beetle

Most beetles eat plants or scraps, but the great diving beetle hunts tadpoles, pond snails, small fish and even baby frogs. It does this as a larva, too. It has to come to the surface for air, which it traps as tiny bubbles under its wing-cases.

Pest beetle quiz – who eats what?

A few beetles cause great damage, usually in their fast-eating grub or larval stage, often called a 'worm'. Can you match these beetle pests with what they eat?

1. Colorado beetles
2. woodworms
3. larder beetles
4. mealworms
5. death-watch beetles

a. potato crops
b. oak beams
c. wooden items such as furniture
d. meat or animal products
e. stored grains (wheat, flour)

answers
1a 2c 3d 4e 5b

Birds

Find out more:
Eggs ▶ Nests ▶

Almost anywhere in the world, you can see birds – flying high, hopping or running, singing or calling, nesting or resting. There are almost 9,000 kinds of bird in every habitat, even icy polar regions. They are all warm-blooded, have feathers and a beak, breed by laying eggs and have wings – but not all can fly.

Word box

down
soft, fluffy feathers of baby birds, also found under the main feathers of adult birds

main wing feathers (primaries)

main flight muscles (pectorals)

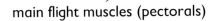

▲ Bird flight

Many birds can fly, in a similar way to this pigeon. Its strong chest muscles pull its wings down, and the broad feathers push air down and back, to lift the bird up and forwards. Smaller shoulder muscles pull the wings up again.

▼ Songs and calls

A bird usually sings to tell other birds to keep out of its territory where it lives and often feeds. The robin's bright red chest feathers also warn other robins: 'Keep out!'. In the breeding season, birds sing to attract partners.

◄ Fast runner

The world's largest bird, the ostrich of Africa, stands over 2 metres tall. It runs fast, at 70 kilometres an hour, but cannot fly. Similar flightless birds are the tall Australian emus, the South American rheas and the smaller, dumpy kiwis of New Zealand.

▶ Eggs and chicks

All birds begin as chicks hatched from eggs. Many parent birds make nests for their eggs, and like this gull, feed and protect their chicks. The chick's down is replaced by brown feathers. A year later it grows the white and grey feathers of an adult gull.

Butterflies and moths

Find out more:
Camouflage ▶ Insects ▶

Most butterflies are colourful and beautiful. Moths are mainly small, grey or brown – but there are exceptions. There are more than 160,000 kinds of these insects, mostly moths, living mainly in tropical forests and grasslands. They all have two pairs of wide, flat wings covered with tiny scales, and eat plants.

Wow!

The most useful moth is the silkmoth. Its caterpillars (called silkworms) spin a covering or cocoon of silk threads that are made into finest silk cloth.

1. butterfly egg

2. caterpillar hatches

3. when fully grown, the caterpillar is ready to turn into a pupa

4. the adult butterfly pushes its way out of the pupa

5. the butterfly spreads and dries its wings

▲ Growing up

All butterflies and moths begin as tiny eggs. These hatch into larvae or caterpillars. When the caterpillar is fully grown it forms a hard body case called a pupa or chrysalis. Eventually, the case splits open and the adult butterfly crawls out. It then dries its wings and can fly after about an hour.

▲ Bright moth

Most moths are small, have hairy bodies, feathery antennae and fly at night. But the zodiac moth of New Guinea is big and bright, with slim antennae and flies by day.

Word box

antennae
feelers found on an insect's head, they are also used to smell

nectar
sweet, sugary liquid made by flowers, to attract insects and other animals

▼ Death's head hawk moth

Most moths hide by day. Their wings are patterned so they blend into their surroundings. But this big, powerful, fast-flying moth has scary markings on its back that look like a human skull!

◄ Pest butterflies and moths

Most adult butterflies and moths sip sweet nectar from flowers. But some of their caterpillars feed on farm crops and cause great damage. White butterfly caterpillars eat cabbages and other vegetables.

Camels

Camels have humps on their backs, which some people think contain water. This is partly true, but the hump really contains body fat, which can be changed into energy and water. This is how a camel can survive weeks in its desert home, without water and food. The camel group includes one-humped dromedaries, two-humped bactrians, non-humped llamas and other cousins from South America.

► Camel cousins

Like their relatives, the camel cousins of South America have long heads, necks and legs, thick fur, and eat tough plants. Smallest is the vicuna of high grasslands in the Andes Mountains. The guanaco is slightly bigger, and lives lower down the mountains.

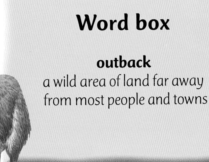

guanaco

Word box

outback
a wild area of land far away from most people and towns

▲ Two humps

The bactrian of Central Asia is well adapted for dry places. It has wide-hoofed feet for walking on soft sand. Its long eyelashes and closeable nostrils keep out dust. It has thick skin and fur to resist hot sun, and tough lips to eat thorny desert plants.

Wow!

Camels are the only animals that run by moving both legs on the same side forward at the same time. It's called pacing and makes the camel sway from side to side — a rocky ride!

► One hump

Dromedaries live mainly in North Africa and the Middle East. Like other camels, they are used for carrying goods and people across dry lands. They also provide milk, meat and skins and are used for racing. Some were taken to Australia for carrying loads and have now become semi-wild in the outback.

Camouflage

Find out more:
Arctic animals ◄ Birds ◄ Fish ► Insects ► Reptiles ►

What makes a polar bear and a vine snake similar? They are both camouflaged – coloured and patterned to blend in with their surroundings. This is common in all kinds of animals, from worms to whales. It helps them to stay unnoticed by predators, or if they are predators themselves, to stay unnoticed by prey (hunted animals)!

▲ Tawny frogmouth

This nocturnal (night) bird rests by day out in the open, relying on its camouflage. It stays perfectly still on a tree or log, its feathers patterned to look like an old, rotting branch stump. It watches through narrow eye-slits – opening its big eyes would get it noticed.

▼ Find the flounder

The sea bed can be made up of pale sand, speckled stones or grey mud. Many flatfish have good camouflage. As this flounder swims about, it slowly changes its colours and patterns to match the sea bed. This prevents its wide body showing up clearly to enemies such as sharks.

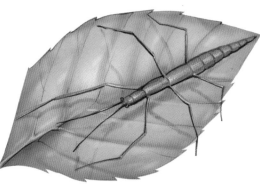

▲ Looks and actions

A creature is often shaped like objects in its surroundings, such as a forest leaf, or seaweed on the shore. The stick insect looks like twigs in trees and bushes, and when the breeze blows, it also sways from side to side, just like them.

Wow!

The fastest quick-colour-change animal is the cuttlefish (cousin of the squid). In a second its whole body can go from almost white to black – or yellow, blue-grey, reddish, even striped!

► Spot the chameleon

The chameleon lizard is famed for its camouflage. Its eyes see the colours around it. They send a message to the brain, which sends signals along nerves to the skin. This makes tiny grains of pigment (coloured substances) spread out or clump together and change the skin colour.

Cats

Find out more:
Desert animals ▶ Grassland animals ▶ Lions and tigers ▶
Mammals ▶ Mountain animals ▶ Swamp animals ▶

Cats are deadly hunters, fast and silent, with strong legs and sharp claws and teeth. All 38 kinds of cats are very similar, differing mainly in size and fur colour. Most wild cats live in forests, have spotted or patched coats and climb trees well. Some survive in deserts. Our pet cats originally came from the African wildcat.

▲ Big cats

The seven big cats are the lion, tiger, cheetah, jaguar, leopard, snow leopard and clouded leopard. The leopard stores a large kill in a tree, away from hyenas and jackals, to eat over several days. It also hunts in towns and raids rubbish for leftover food.

Word scramble

Unscramble these words to find the names of five types of cat:

a. TACLIWD
b. MUPA
c. REGIT
d. TOLECO
e. HATEECH

answers
a. wildcat b. puma
c. tiger d. ocelot e. cheetah

▼ Fast cats

Most cats run fast in bursts, but cannot keep going as dogs do. The cheetah is the world's fastest runner, reaching up to 100 kilometres an hour, but for less than 30 seconds.

Wow!

The smallest cat is the black-footed cat of southern Africa, which is half the size of many pet cats.

◀ Cold cats

Cats shed their fur and grow a new coat once or twice each year. The lynx's winter coat is pale and thick. Like most wild cats, the lynx is now rare. People kill it for its fur, or in case it attacks farm animals or humans.

▲ Lazy cats

The bobcat, named after its short 'bobbed' tail, is a medium-sized cat from North America. Cats tend to live alone, hunt at night and sleep by day. Many have dens in hollow trees, under logs or in caves.

Cattle

Some cattle graze peacefully in farm meadows – but others may battle with tigers in swamps or with wolves on the prairie. There are about 12 kinds of cattle, such as cows, oxen and buffalo. Half are truly wild. Of the others, such as the yak, gaur and water buffalo, a few are wild but most are kept by people. They are all big, heavy plant-eaters, with horns.

▶ Indian cattle

The gaur or Indian bison has a massive body with humped shoulders. Like most cattle it needs a daily drink and sometimes wallows in mud to get rid of flies and other pests. Other cattle of South and Southeast Asia include the mountain anoa, lowland anoa, banteng, kouprey and tamarua.

gaur

▲ African buffalo

Few wild cattle are as 'wild' as this buffalo, which charges without warning. It often kills the animal that is chasing it. The males bellow, snort, stamp and bang heads during the breeding season. The winner can mate with the females.

Wow!

One of the world's rarest big animals is the kouprey or wild forest ox of Southeast Asia. There are just a hundred or so left – if that.

▼ Not a 'buffalo'

One of the biggest wild cattle, the male North American bison, stands 2 metres at the shoulder and weighs 1 tonne. These bison were almost wiped out by 'Wild West' European hunters, but herds now roam the range again – although they are far fewer in number.

Courtship

Courtship is what creatures perform before they mate and produce young. In most animals, a female and male of the same kind come together to breed. In courtship, each checks that a possible partner is fit, healthy and ready to be a parent. Often it involves sights, sounds, smells and actions.

► Look at me, peahen!

Usually it's the male animal who puts on a courting display to impress the female. This peacock spreads his long tail feathers as a graceful fan. He shakes this with a rattling noise, calls loudly and struts about.

▲ Getting together

Animals court in many different ways. Grasshoppers chirp, butterflies flap wings, sharks bite each other and crabs lock pincers. This female and male Cape gannet use their long beaks like swords to 'fence'. But the aim is staying together rather than fighting.

dusky titi

▲ Strong bond

In the Amazon rainforest, the female and male dusky titi stay together, not just during courtship, but all year. Each dawn they sit side by side on a branch, wrap their tails together and sing loudly.

Wow!

The courting 'love song' of the male humpback whale travels more than 100 kilometres through the ocean.

Who does which courtship?

Can you match each male animal to his style of courtship?

1. hangs from a branch, shakes his wings and tail and sings loudly
2. swims around the female showing a bright red belly
3. croaks loudly and jumps on the female's back
4. coils around and rubs the female

a. viper **b.** bird of paradise **c.** stickleback **d.** frog

1b 2c 3d 4a
answers

Crabs and other crustaceans

Find out more:
Seashore animals ▶
Shellfish ▶

Crustaceans are 'insects of the sea'. Like insects on land, they swarm in the oceans in billions. There are over 40,000 kinds including crabs, lobsters, prawns, shrimps, krill (which look like shrimps) and barnacles on seashore rocks. Copepods and branchiopods are smaller and more rounded, and even more numerous. They include a few freshwater types like the pond 'water flea', daphnia.

Wow!

The largest crustacean is the giant spider crab. Its body is as big as a dinner-plate and its long legs and pincers would hang over the edge of a double bed!

▶ On the march

Some crustaceans migrate (travel) with the tides or seasons. These spiny lobsters are marching to deeper water to breed.

▼ Crustaceans on land

A few crustaceans, like the wood-louse (sowbug), survive on land, far from the sea. Even so, they need to stay in cool, damp places, such as under bark or logs, or they dry out and die.

▼ Tough customer

The robber crab is big, strong and fierce, with pincers the size of your hands. Like many crabs and other crustaceans, it feeds by scavenging on old, rotting bits and pieces of almost anything. This crab lives mainly on the shore, and can even climb trees.

◀ Non-crusty crustacean

Most crustaceans have a hard outer body casing, one or more sets of antennae (feelers), at least four pairs of legs, and perhaps strong pincers. The hermit crab is unusually soft-bodied. It finds an empty whelk or similar shell and hides safely inside it.

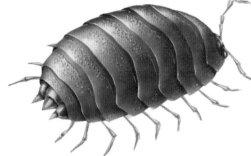

Crocodiles and alligators

Find out more:
Baby animals ◄ Reptiles ►
River and lake animals ►

Crocodiles have survived from the age of dinosaurs – but in some cases, only just. There are 23 types of crocodiles and their cousins – alligators, caimans and gharial (gavial). All are powerful meat-eaters, catching prey or scavenging on dead meat. But some have been hunted by people for meat and skins, or because they threaten us or our animals.

▼ Biggest reptile

The largest crocodile, and biggest reptile, is the saltwater or estuarine crocodile. Most crocodiles live in fresh water along rivers, lakes and swamps, but this massive beast swims along coasts and even out to sea. It lives along the shores of South and Southeast Asia and Australia.

▲ Chinese alligator

One of the smallest and rarest types, the Chinese alligator is only 2 metres long. Its prey is also small – water snails, worms and the occasional water rat or duck. During the winter it hibernates out of water, in a cave or den, waking up in the warmth of spring.

Wow!

Crocodiles are among the longest-lived animals. Some survive to well over 100 years of age.

► Teeth and scales

A crocodile's pointed, well-spaced teeth grip all kinds of prey, including fish, birds and mammals. The body is covered with hard, bony scales. As old teeth and scales wear and fall off, new ones take their place.

Deep sea animals

At the bottom of the sea, every day is the same – and night too. It's always dark, cold and still, with huge pressure. Below about 500 metres there is no light, and so no plants. Animals survive on bits of food sinking down from above – or eat each other. There are glow-in-the-dark fish, squid, strange-shaped crabs, shellfish, starfish, sea urchins, sea cucumbers, sea lilies and giant worms galore!

▲ Big-mouthed eel

The gulper eel, about 60 centimetres long, is also called the black swallower. Its flexible mouth can swallow an animal twice its size. Many deep-sea creatures are black. Colours and patterns are of no use in the darkness. Some have no eyes at all.

▶ Fanged fish

The deep sea is the world's biggest habitat. But food is quite scarce, so relatively few animals live there. Most are small – the viperfish is hardly longer than your hand. It has long fangs, like a snake, to grab any possible passing meal.

◀ Deep-sea anglerfish

This wide-mouthed, sharp-toothed hunter 'fishes' for prey with its long front fin spine, which has a glowing tip. Small creatures are lured by this light in the darkness, and the angler swallows them whole.

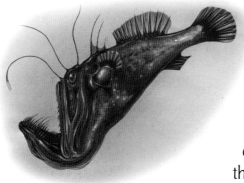

Word box

fang
a long, thin, sharp-pointed tooth

pressure
a pushing or pressing force, measured over a certain area such as a square centimetre

tubeworms

▶ Deep-sea tubeworms

Here and there on the sea bed, hot water rich in minerals, from deep in the Earth, spurts out through cracks. Microbes and tiny creatures thrive on the minerals, and they become food for bigger crabs, blind fish and tubeworms larger than your arm. It is a warm, food-rich 'island' on the vast, cold, muddy ocean floor.

Deer

Find out more:
Antelopes and gazelles ◄ Cattle ◄
Horses and zebras ► Mammals ►

Male deer spend most of the year growing their impressive antlers on the head. When these fall off, a new set starts to grow. Deer are hoofed, plant-eating mammals with keen senses. Most of the 45 different kinds live wild in woods and forests. Some deer are kept in parks or as herds for meat, milk or skins and become quite tame. Others are hunted in the wild.

Wow!

The reindeer, or caribou, is the only kind of deer where the female has antlers, as well as the male.

Chinese water deer

▲ Small deer

The smallest deer include muntjac, Chinese water deer (where neither sex has antlers) and chevrotains or mouse deer. Some are hardly bigger than rabbits. They lead secretive lives in thick forests, either alone or in small groups.

moose or elk

red deer

◄ Big deer

The biggest deer is called a moose in North America and an elk in Europe. A large male stands 2 metres at the shoulder and has antlers 2 metres across. Another large deer is called a red deer in Europe and a wapiti in North America and East Asia.

Word scramble

Unscramble these words to find the names of five types of deer:

a. WOLLAF
b. ERO
c. KISA
d. MABRAS
e. KEL

answers
a. fallow b. roe
c. sika d. sambar e. elk

▼ Deer herd

Most deer live in herds (groups) made up of hinds (females) with fawns (young) and separate stags or bucks (males). These white-tailed bucks are from North America. At breeding time the males bellow, stamp and clash antlers (rutting). The winner takes over the female herd for a time, to breed.

Desert animals

The world's deserts are dry, harsh places, but only about one-fifth are scorching sand. Most are stony or rocky, and some are freezing cold, especially at night. Yet animals survive here – especially scorpions, beetles and other insects, reptiles like lizards and snakes, and birds that can fly far to find water and food.

▲ Thorny devil

The moloch, or thorny devil, lives in Australia's 'Red Centre'. It walks slowly and unafraid, protected by its totally prickly body, and licks up ants and termites. At night, it dips its head low, and dew collects on its body and trickles into its mouth.

▼ Eat anything

The tall, flightless emu is Australia's 'eat-anything' bird. It pecks up leaves, thorny plants, dry grass, seeds, roots, grubs and small animals. Emus live in groups, deep in the dry outback. Sometimes they raid farm fields and have to be culled.

▲ Tough toad

Most amphibians need water, but a few are adapted to dryness. Spadefoot toads live in many deserts. They have thick skin and a wedgelike part on the foot, for digging. By day they hide in the soil, where it is cooler and damp. When the rare rains arrive, they breed quickly in puddles.

▼ Caracal

The caracal or desert lynx survives in the world's biggest desert, the Sahara of Africa. It hunts ground animals such as wild pigs and can spring 3 metres into the air to grab low-flying birds.

Word box

cull
controlling the number of animals by killing them for a very good reason, such as preserving their own habitat

Dolphins

Dolphins seem to have great fun as they swim, leap and play among the waves. But each year millions get caught in fishing nets and drown. There are 32 types. These include pilot whales and six river dolphins, which live in fresh water. The six types of porpoises have much blunter snouts. They all have teeth and hunt fish or squid. Most live in schools or pods (groups), and communicate with squeals and clicks.

Wow!

Hector's dolphin is sometimes called the Mickey Mouse dolphin, because its dorsal (back) fin is shaped like this famous cartoon character's ears!

◀ The largest dolphin

The largest dolphin is one of the world's biggest predators – the killer whale, or orca. A big male is almost 10 metres long and 10 tonnes in weight. Some pods of orcas hunt mainly fish in one area, while others wander and prefer seals.

▲ Blunt-beaked dolphin

Risso's dolphin is one of the larger types, measuring about 4 metres in length. Like most dolphins it has smooth, sleek skin, two flippers, a dorsal fin and curved tail flukes. It also has an unusually short beak.

▶ Baby dolphins

Dolphins are mammals and breathe air through the blowhole on the top of their head. A baby dolphin is born underwater and nudged to the surface by its mother, for breaths of air. A calf, like this spinner dolphin, swims close to its mother.

Ducks and swans

Find out more:
Birds ◄ Migrating animals ►
River and lake animals ►

In almost any river or lake, you will find colourful, quacking, flapping, paddling waterfowl – ducks, geese and swans. There are 150 different kinds, all strong fliers with webbed feet. They peck, dabble or up-end with their wide beaks, feeding on water plants, grass, seeds, and sometimes small animals such as pond snails, worms and grubs.

Word box

dabble
when waterfowl feed by opening and closing the beak quickly at the water's surface

up-end
when waterfowl feed by poking the head and neck under the water, with the tail sticking up

▼ Canada geese

People have taken these geese from their North American home, across Europe and even to New Zealand. Like many geese, in some regions they journey or migrate northwards to breed in summer. They then return south to warmer regions in winter.

▲ Black swan

Waterfowl, also known as wildfowl, can be quite tame. The black swan, originally from Australia, has been taken to many new regions to brighten up lakes and parks. Its wings are more than 2 metres across and it has a very long neck – even for a swan!

▼ Mute swan

Most waterfowl build large, untidy nests along river and lake banks. The mute swan hen (female) gives her babies piggyback rides from the nest, as they quickly learn to swim and feed. The cob (male) stays nearby to guard them.

◄ Shelduck

Shelducks like shallow, salty water along seashores, coastal lagoons and salt pans. They search in the mud for shellfish and worms. The most common duck is the mallard. Others include eiders, scoters, teals, wigeons, pintails, shovelers, scaups and smews.

Eagles and hawks

Eagles, hawks and falcons are the great predators of the skies.
There are more than 300 kinds of birds of prey, or raptors, from huge American condors with 3-metre wings to tiny falconets and kestrels hardly bigger than blackbirds.

Wow!
The peregrine falcon moves faster than any other animal when it power-dives or 'stoops' onto prey at 220 kilometres an hour.

▲ International hunter

The osprey or fish-eagle is the most widespread raptor, found on all lands except the far north and Antarctica. Like most raptors, it hunts by day using its incredible eyesight, soaring and gliding until it spots a fish just under the surface.

▶ Feet for fishing

All birds of prey have sharp, hooked beaks and sharp, curved talons (claws). The osprey's talons are especially sharp, and its toes are spiny underneath, to grip slippery fish as it hurls itself feet-first into the water.

osprey talon

▼ Gyrfalcon

The largest falcon is the gyrfalcon, which hunts over Arctic ice and snow. It swoops low and catches mainly birds, such as ptarmigan and willow grouse, plus occasional lemmings and voles. As with many raptors, the male and female make amazing courtship flights as they dive, climb, roll and loop in the air.

◄ Golden eagle

The female and male golden eagle build a big, untidy nest of twigs, high on a tree, cliff or crag. They may have several nests, called eyries, using one each year and adding more twigs each time.

Egg-laying mammals

Most mammal females give birth to babies. But there are five kinds of mammals that are egg-layers – these are called monotremes. One of these is the duck-billed platypus from eastern Australia. The other four are echidnas (spiny anteaters) from Australia and New Guinea. Echidnas have sharp spines as well as fur. They have huge claws to dig for ants, termites, grubs and worms, which they lick up with their spiny tongues.

egg in pouch

▼ How the platypus lives

The platypus lives along rivers and billabongs. At night it noses in the mud for worms, shellfish and other small animals. The male has a spur on his rear ankle, which he uses to jab poison into enemies.

Wow!

The young platypus has a long journey as it leaves its nursery burrow to see daylight for the first time – the burrow may be more than 30 metres long.

▲ Echidna and egg

The short-beaked echidna rests in her burrow, holding her egg warm and safe in a slitlike pouch. This develops on her belly only at breeding time. The egg grows in her body for 23 days, then develops in her pouch for 10 days. After hatching, the baby stays in the pouch for another seven weeks, then in a nest burrow for six months.

Word box

billabong
Australian native word meaning 'dead water', used for a natural pool or small lake

spur
sharp claw or clawlike part on the foot or ankle of some animals, especially birds

Eggs

Find out more:
Amphibians ◄ Baby animals ◄ Birds ◄ Egg-laying mammals ◄
Fish ► Insects ► Reptiles ►

Most female animals lay tough-shelled eggs. This includes all birds, nearly all reptiles, fish, insects, spiders and other creatures. Each egg contains a tiny young animal, called an embryo, which grows and develops into a baby. When ready, it bites or tears its way out of the shell – and then often faces the world alone.

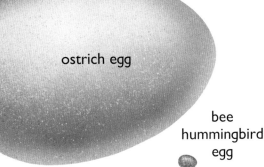

ostrich egg

bee hummingbird egg

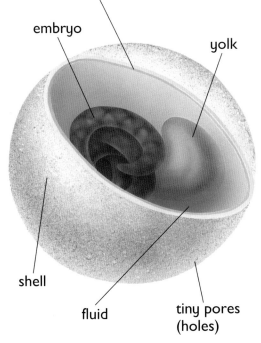

shell membrane (lining)

embryo

yolk

shell

fluid

tiny pores (holes)

▲ Inside an egg

A typical egg has a tough outer case or shell for protection. Inside is a store of yolk to nourish the tiny developing animal, or embryo, which floats in a pool of fluid for protection. Oxygen, the substance that all animals need to breathe, passes to the embryo through tiny pores in the shell.

▲ Size and number

The ostrich lays the largest eggs – 16 centimetres long and over 3,000 times heavier than the tiny egg of the bee hummingbird. The kiwi lays a single egg, one-quarter the size of its body. The ling fish lays more than 20 million tiny eggs.

Wow!

Small creatures called fairy shrimps have hatched out of eggs that were wetted again, after being dried and preserved for more than 2,000 years.

▼ Slimy eggs

Bird eggs have hard, rigid shells. Most other eggs have slightly flexible, leathery shells. Frog and toad eggs, called spawn, are covered with slimy jelly. Frog spawn is clumped, while toad spawn is in long strings or 'necklaces'.

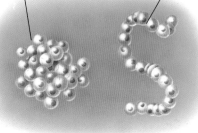

frog spawn

toad spawn

▼ Hidden eggs

Many reptiles, such as this African dwarf crocodile, dig a hole and then cover the eggs with old plants. As the plants rot they create heat. This incubates the eggs (keeps them warm) and helps them develop.

Elephants

No other animal looks like the elephant, with its long trunk, large tusks and huge ears. Asian elephants and African forest elephants live mainly in woods, while African savanna elephants live on grasslands. All are under threat, shot for their ivory tusks or because they destroy farm crops. Some Asian elephants are tame and carry logs for people or let them ride on their backs.

► Asian elephant

This elephant is slightly smaller than the African types and has smaller-sized ears. An elephant's trunk is its nose and top lip joined together. It uses it to grasp food, suck up water to squirt in its mouth, sniff the air and stroke babies and friends in the herd.

▲ African elephant

Most African savanna elephants have tusks. Tusks are huge incisor teeth, made of ivory. They are used to dig for food, push down trees for their leaves, fruits and bark, for defence against enemies and to fight rival males at breeding time.

rock hyraxes

◄ Small cousins

The closest relations to elephants are the hyraxes of Africa and the Middle East. Rock hyraxes are found in dry, rocky places. Tree hyraxes are found in branches. They all live in groups and eat plants.

Word scramble

Unscramble these words to find the names of five types of elephant food:

a. SAGRS
b. KARB
c. SEVLEA
d. STURIF
e. STORO

answers
a. grass b. bark
c. leaves d. fruits e. roots

▼ Living in herds

A herd contains mothers and calves (young). 'Aunts' without young help with calf-care. An older female, the matriarch, leads the herd to traditional feeding places and waterholes.

Endangered animals

Find out more:
Lions and tigers ▶ Rhinos and tapirs ▶
Turtles and tortoises ▶

Hundreds of mammals, birds, reptiles and other animals are under threat. They are killed for their meat, fur, feathers or skins, or killed as 'sport' trophies. They are also accidentally harmed by pollution, or caught in nets and traps. But the single greatest threat they face is habitat destruction.

▼ Tourist trouble

Dolphins, and sea turtles such as leatherbacks, get trapped in fishing nets and drown. Turtles are also threatened by tourism. Quiet beaches, where they lay eggs under cover of darkness, are invaded by hotels, bright lights and noisy nightlife.

leatherback turtle

Word box

conservation
protection of the natural world

habitat destruction
ruining the natural places where animals live by using them for farming, houses, roads and industry

◀ Ancient fish

The coelacanth became famous in 1938, when a specimen was caught off east Africa. Until then scientists had thought this primitive-looking fish had died out 70 million years ago.

Conservation – how we can help

• Support organizations that help wildlife
• Join campaigns to save natural regions and wild places
• Help research and captive breeding projects – for example, 'adopt an animal'
• Buy products that are environmentally friendly
• Waste less and recycle more
• Encourage people to care for wildlife

▶ Giant panda

This bamboo-eating bear is the famous symbol of conservation. Maybe fewer than 1,000 pandas now live wild in China. Like whales, gorillas and other large animals, pandas breed slowly, having only one or two young, several years apart.

Farm animals

Animals are kept on farms for doing work and providing milk, skins, fur, feathers, scales and meat. Farm animals include chickens, cows, sheep, and pigs, and more unusual ones, such as llamas, camels, reindeer, rabbits, guinea-pigs, pigeons, ostriches, salmon, and even snakes and crocodiles!

► Chicken

The world has more chickens than people. There are at least 500 different breeds and they provide one-third of all our meat, plus trillions of eggs. But some are not kept for practical use. They are 'fancy fowl' with bright colours and extraordinary feathers, bred to win prizes at shows.

▼ The 'recycling' pig

About half the world's one billion pigs are in south and east Asia. They eat anything from roots and fruits to grubs, worms and scraps, and are farmed for their meat – pork, bacon and ham.

▼ Milk for all

People have kept farm animals, such as cows, by selective breeding from their wild ancestors to produce the things we need. The cow gives tasty meat, tough skin for leather, and plenty of milk – not only to feed her calf, but for us, all year round.

Word box

ancestor
a relative from long ago, like a great-great-grandparent

selective breeding
choosing animals with certain features (like long fur) to breed together, so the features are greater in their offspring (such as even longer fur)

◄ Special breeds

Goats were first herded almost 10,000 years ago. There are dozens of different breeds, each with special features. Angora goats have fleeces (woolly coats) of fine, white, silky fur. It is shorn (cut off) and woven into mohair cloth.

Fish

Find out more:
Camouflage ◄ Fliers and gliders ► Nests ► Pets ► Poisonous animals ►
River and lake animals ► Sea animals ► Sharks ►

shoal of yellow snappers

There are almost 25,000 different types of fish. They range from massive ocean sharks to catfish and carp in weedy lakes, salmon and trout leaping in fast rivers, tiny minnows in puddles and slimy eels on the sea bed. All fish have gills (feathery parts used for breathing). Most have fins, a tail for swimming and scales on the body.

barracuda

▲ Fish and people

Salmon, trout and other fish are farmed in ponds or giant sea cages. Tuna, cod, herring, mackerel and other ocean fish are caught in huge nets, to provide food for people, pets and farm animals.

Word box

edible
able to be eaten

fry
baby fish,
just hatched from eggs

▲ Fierce fish

Different fish eat many kinds of foods. Barracudas in the sea, and pike and piranhas in lakes, are sharp-toothed hunters of other creatures. Carp and mullet search in the mud for any edible bits. On coral reefs, parrotfish scrape tiny bits of coral and seaweed off rocks, while angelfish feast on tough sponges.

▼ Father fish

In most fish, the female casts her eggs into the water and they get no further care. But the seahorse puts her eggs into a 'pocket' on her male partner's front. They develop into fry here and are then 'born'.

male seahorse

Wow!

The fastest fish is probably the sailfish, which surges along at 105 kilometres an hour – as fast as a cheetah runs.

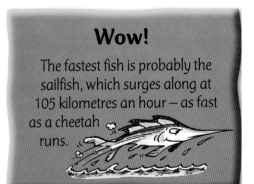

Flamingos and wading birds

Find out more:
Birds ◀
Ducks and swans ◀

As you paddle in the sea or lake, there are probably birds doing the same. There are over 400 types of waders or shorebirds. Most have very long legs, to walk in deep water without getting too wet, and long necks and bills, to reach down and peck in sand or mud for food such as worms.

Wow!

Flamingos can wade and feed in very salty, shallow lakes where the water is hotter than in our bathtubs.

◀ Scarlet ibis

In northern parts of South America, these brilliant birds gather in huge flocks and, unusually for waders, build their nests in trees. They probe deeply in mud with their long bills, finding food mainly by touch.

▼ Catching oysters

Waders, such as the oyster-catcher, do not have webbed toes. Oyster-catchers are widespread across Europe and Asia, along lakes and seas. The bill has a chisel-shaped end which can easily crack open tough-shelled sea food.

Word box

bill
a bird's beak (other animals like dolphins and octopus have 'beaks' but these are not called bills)

webbed
toes (or fingers) joined by flaps of thin skin, usually for swimming

▲ Going fishing

Most herons stand tall, wade slowly, then stay very still as they watch for fish, frogs and insects. But some, like this green-backed heron, 'go fishing'. They drop small bits of food into the water to attract fish, which the heron then grabs with its dagger-sharp bill.

▲ Longest legs and neck

Flamingos are the tallest waders, about 150 centimetres high. They live in large flocks. A flamingo feeds in water by holding its bill upside down and 'combing' tiny animals and plants with brushlike parts inside its bill.

Fliers and gliders

Find out more:
Bats ◀ Fish ◀ Squirrels ▶
Tropical forest animals ▶

Only bats, birds and insects can truly fly.
Many other groups of animals have a few types that can glide, swoop, soar or float. There are 'flying' spiders, fish, frogs, snakes, lizards, possums and squirrels. Most have wide, flat body surfaces that work like parachutes, but cannot be flapped like real wings.

Word box

pectoral
to do with the shoulder region, at the front or upper side of the body

Wow!

Sometimes a gust of wind lifts a flying fish so high, it lands on the deck of a boat — and cannot take off again.

▼ Furry gliders

American flying squirrels have a furry flap of skin along each side, stretched by holding out the legs. The squirrel steers by tilting its flattened tail. Like other squirrels, it is an expert climber and eats nuts, fruits and juicy bark.

▲ Flying fish

These fishes' 'wings' are its pectoral fins. The flying fish leaps out of the water at up to 50 kilometres an hour. It swoops for up to 100 metres, usually to avoid a predator such as a marlin or shark.

▲ Flying frog

The amazing flying frog of the Southeast Asian rainforests has large webs of skin between its toes, for gliding and swimming. It also has narrow skin flaps along its legs. It lives in trees and lays its eggs in a leaf.

◀ Super glider

The 'flying lemur' is not a lemur but a colugo, a plant-eating mammal from the Southeast Asian rainforest treetops. It is the best mammal glider after bats and has thin, stretchy skin flaps all around its body. It can easily glide 100 metres, and on a breezy day, land higher up than it took off.

Flies

It's hard to ignore a buzzing housefly, blood-sucking mosquito, hovering hoverfly or painful-biting horsefly. There are over 120,000 kinds of fly. A fly has only two wings, unlike most other flying insects, such as bees and butterflies, which have four. Flies live in almost every habitat and eat every kind of food, from flowers and fruits to blood, rotting flesh, dung and other flies.

housefly

▶ Housefly

Some flies have sharp, pointed mouths for sucking up liquids. The housefly has a spongy tip to its tubelike mouth. It dribbles saliva onto food, which turns it into a 'soup', then sucks it up. Like most flies, it has small feelers and big eyes.

◀ Scorpion fly

The scorpion fly does not have a tail sting. The tail end is specialized for mating in the male or laying eggs in the female. Nor is it a true fly. It is one of many insects called a 'fly' – because it does just that.

Wow!

Some midges, which are tiny kinds of true flies, beat their wings over 1,000 times every second.

▶ Fruit fly

Some flies are pests. Fruit flies gather around ripe and rotting fruit in autumn and can ruin farms and orchards. But these flies can be useful, too. Much of what we know about our genes, has come from studies of fruit flies.

▼ Dragonfly fly-eater

With four wings, the dragonfly is not a true fly. It is very fast and acrobatic as it hunts gnats and midges. Other insect fliers that are not real flies are stoneflies, alderflies, caddisflies, mayflies and sawflies.

dragonfly

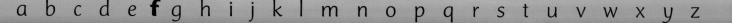

Frogs and toads

Find out more:
Amphibians ◄ Desert animals ◄
Eggs ◄ Fliers and gliders ◄

There are more than 4,200 types of tail-less amphibians around the world. These are frogs and toads. Frogs have smooth, moist skin, slim bodies and long legs and tend to leap, while toads have drier, lumpy skin, tubby bodies and shorter legs and usually waddle.

▼ Frog face

The American bullfrog has large, bulging eyes to see prey and a wide, toothless mouth to grab it. It also has a round eardrum to hear well – especially the croaks of other frogs at mating time. Usually only males call out, to attract females and frighten off rival males.

eardrum

▼ Horns like thorns

The strange points over the Malaysian horned frog's eyes resemble plant thorns. Like many frogs it has long rear legs for jumping, and a long, sticky-tipped tongue that it flicks out to grab prey.

Word scramble

Unscramble these words to find the names of four types of frogs and toads:

a. RETE GROF
b. PEDASTOOF ADOT
c. ENERG OGRF
d. NEDROH OTDA

answers
a. tree frog b. spadefoot toad c. green frog d. horned toad

► African bullfrog

Big and strong, this bullfrog eats many creatures, including snakes, lizards and other frogs. The male guards the eggs (spawn) that the female lays, and he also protects the tadpoles when they hatch.

▲ Giant toad

The giant, marine or cane toad has a head and body 25 centimetres long. Like most frogs and toads, it puffs itself up and hisses when in danger. Its skin makes a poison that can kill predators.

Giraffes

Why are giraffes like our fingerprints? Because no two have exactly the same pattern. The brown patches and creamy lines vary from one giraffe to another. They help the giraffe to blend in with the patchy shade of leafy branches in the grassy woods of Africa. Each giraffe roams around a home area, usually with others of its kind.

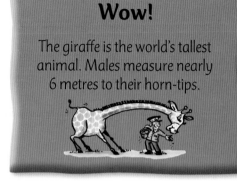

▼ Giraffe herd

Male giraffes breed after winning 'necking' contests with rivals, bashing their necks together. A female leaves the group to give birth to the world's tallest baby, at 2 metres high. Most giraffes visit a waterhole at dawn or dusk, splay their front legs and lower their long necks to drink. They are rarely attacked — an adult giraffe can kill a lion with one kick of its dinner-plate-sized hoof.

▼ Okapi

The only close relative of the giraffe is the okapi, a rare and shy creature of central African forests. It looks like a combination of giraffe and zebra, lives alone, and eats leaves and fruits. Its horns are like the giraffe's, but only the male has them.

▼ Curly tongue

The giraffe's very long, powerful tongue grasps a twigful of leaves and pulls this into the mouth. Then the head jerks away so the teeth take the leaves off the twigs.

Grassland animals

Find out more:
Cats ◄ Cattle ◄ Horses and zebras ►

Grasslands form where there is not enough rain for trees, but too much for a desert. Tall, waving plants are food for a huge variety of animals, from tiny termites and lizards, to huge grazers like bison on the North American prairies, and zebras and elephants on African savannas.

► Champion digger

The African aardvark is active at night. It uses its big ears and long snout to find ants and termites, then digs them out with its massive front claws, and licks them up with its sticky, long tongue.

▲ Striding birds

Many tall, flightless birds live on grasslands. The 1.5-metre-tall secretary bird of Africa can fly but prefers to stride along, covering 30 kilometres daily. It eats small animals such as insects, mice, birds and snakes, which it kills by stamping and pecking.

► Spotted serval

Africa has several grassland cats, including the cheetah, the fastest runner of all animals. The serval is like a small cheetah, with long legs and spotted fur to blend in with its surroundings. It catches and eats many creatures, including baby antelopes and low-flying birds.

serval

Word scramble

Unscramble these words to find the names of five types of grassland habitat:

a. WODEMA (Europe)
b. AIRPIRE (North America)
c. PEPSET (Asia)
d. SAPMAP (South America)
e. VANANAS (Africa)

a. meadow b. prairie
c. steppe d. pampas e. savanna
answers

Hedgehogs and moles

Hedgehogs, moles, desmans and shrews are all insectivores. They are a group of about 370 kinds of mammals – mostly small, sharp-toothed animals who eat insects as well as other bugs, grubs, worms and creepy-crawlies.

▲ Hog in the hedge

The European hedgehog is named after its piglike snorts as it noses for small creatures in hedgerows, woods and meadows. It can roll into a prickly ball, protected by its 5,000 sharp spines. Like most insectivores, it usually lives alone.

desman

▼ Digging machine

A mole's front paws are massive, with wide claws like a spade to burrow through soil. Each mole digs a long network of tunnels. It lives in a chamber called a fortress with a molehill above.

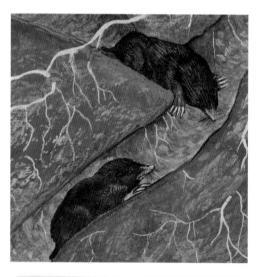

Wow!

The smallest land mammal is the pygmy white-toothed shrew, whose head and body is just 4 centimetres long – its tail is half this length.

▲ Diving desman

The insectivore group includes moonrats in Asia, solenodons in the West Indies and tenrecs in Africa. They are all shrewlike, with long whiskers, quivering noses and quick movements. The desmans of West Europe and Asia have part-webbed feet. They catch fish, grubs and worms in fast streams.

◄ Shrews

There are 250 types of shrew all around the world. They range in size from smaller than your thumb, to the size of a rat. They all hunt creatures sometimes bigger than themselves. The smallest shrews have to eat a big meal every eight hours or they starve.

Word box

insectivore
insect-eater, although insectivores often eat many other types of small animal

quivering
shaking

Hibernating animals

Find out more:
Bats ◄ Crocodiles and alligators ◄
Rodents ► Squirrels ►

Before the start of a long, cold winter, some animals fall into a deep sleep, called hibernation. This helps them get through a long, cold and harsh winter when there is very little food. An animal that hibernates cannot wake up, even if it tries, until its hibernation ends.

◄ A special day

The groundhog is a large North American ground squirrel. Tradition tells how it peers from its burrow on Groundhog Day, 2 February, to see if it is warm enough to stop hibernating. In fact, it usually hibernates until March.

▼ Who hibernates?

Mammals that hibernate include bats, hedgehogs and various kinds of rodents, such as mice, rats, marmots and some squirrels. In autumn they feast and store energy as fat in their bodies, to survive for their months asleep.

squirrel

bats hibernate in hollow trees or caves, where it is cold but rarely freezing

the dormouse hibernates in a snug nest of leaves, moss and twigs, among tree roots

hedgehog

Word box

sett
the underground tunnels and chambers that are home to a badger family

badgers in their sett

Horses and zebras

Find out more:
Farm animals ◄ Grassland animals ◄
Mammals ► Pets ►

The horse's cousins include three kinds of zebras in Africa and two kinds of wild asses in Africa and Asia. Over 100 years ago, before cars and trucks were invented, horses were widely used for pulling loads and carrying people.

Wow!

The wild horse no longer lives wild. It is rare and kept mainly in parks and nature reserves.

► Asses and donkeys

A few wild asses still roam dry areas in northeast Africa, the Middle East and central Asia. They survive great heat. Donkeys are domesticated versions of asses. They were tamed by people more than 5,000 years ago in the Middle East to be strong and carry heavy loads.

donkey

▼ Species of horses

All domesticated horses belong to the same group or species – from massive and powerful heavy horses such as shires to agile polo ponies, often used for playing polo, a ball game. Horses have been bred by people for different jobs for more than 4,000 years.

Word scramble

Unscramble these words to find the names of five breeds or types of horses:

a. HOCARERSE
b. SHRIE EROHS
c. RETHUN
d. STUMNAG
e. NIMOLOPA

answers
a. racehorse b. Shire horse c. hunter d. mustang e. palomino

heavy horse

polo pony

◄ Zebras

Like all horses and their relatives, zebras eat mainly grass. They have long legs, each with one large toe, capped by a hard hoof. Their keen senses detect distant danger and they can race away at more than 60 kilometres an hour. Each group or herd consists of mares (females) and foals (young), led by a stallion (adult male).

Insects

Find out more:
Animal societies ◄ Beetles ◄ Butterflies and moths ◄ Flies ◄
Pests ►

Nine out of every ten animals we know about are insects. They are among the most widespread of all animals. Some are helpful, like silkmoths and honey bees, and dung beetles which recycle animal droppings. Others are harmful. Flies carry germs, locusts destroy crops, wasps can sting, and mosquitoes spread diseases.

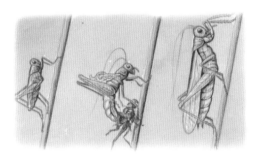

▲ Changing shape

When it grows, the young insect or larva moults its hard outer casing, then a new one rapidly grows and hardens. Most larvae, like this cricket, look similar to the adult and are called nymphs.

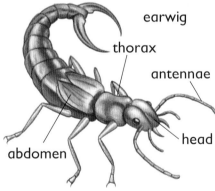

earwig
thorax
antennae
head
abdomen

▲ Insect features

An insect has three distinct body parts. The head has antennae, eyes and mouth-parts. The thorax has six legs and, usually, four wings. The abdomen contains the guts and reproductive parts.

▼ Lonely insects?

Most insects live alone, meeting others of their kind only to mate. Some, like cockroaches and aphids (greenflies), gather in groups. Most bees, wasps, ants and termites are social insects. They live in groups and work together.

bee

▶ No sting

The wood-wasp's tail looks like a sting, but it is actually just a tube for the female to lay her eggs. Wood-wasp larvae eat timber and are sometimes called wood-worms.

Main groups of insects

- Alderflies and dobsonflies
- Aphids, hoppers, bedbugs and other bugs
- Bees, wasps, sawflies and ants
- Beetles and weevils
- Bristletails and silverfish (no wings)
- Butterflies and moths
- Caddisflies
- Cockroaches
- Dragonflies and damselflies
- Earwigs
- Fleas
- Grasshoppers, crickets, locusts and katydids
- Houseflies, craneflies, gnats, mosquitoes and other flies (two wings only)
- Lacewings and antlions
- Lice
- Mayflies
- Praying mantises and mantids
- Scorpionflies
- Snakeflies
- Stick insects and leaf insects
- Stoneflies
- Termites
- Thrips and thunderbugs

garden tiger moth

wood-wasp

cricket

One of the world's speediest animals bounds along on its huge back feet at more than 50 kilometres an hour – the red kangaroo. At almost 2 metres tall, it is the largest of about 50 kinds of kangaroos and smaller wallabies. These marsupial mammals live in Australia, with a few in Papua New Guinea.

◀ Boomers and fliers

A big male red kangaroo, or 'boomer', can clear a fence 3 metres tall. Many red kangaroos vary in colour from cream to rusty brown. They live in groups in the outback and gather at waterholes during drought.

▼ Boxing kangaroos

Male kangaroos push, pull and wrestle with their arms, and may kick out with their great feet, using the strong tail for support. They are battling for females at breeding time.

▲ Wallaby

There are many kinds of wallabies, with names such as wallaroos, pademelons, bettongs and prettyfaces. Some live in forests, while others prefer rocky scrub or grassy plains. Like kangaroos, they use their tail for balance when bounding and to lean on at rest.

Wow!

Some kangaroos live in trees! Tree kangaroos dwell in forests in Papua New Guinea and northeast Australia and have grasping hands and padded feet.

Word box

drought
a long, dry period with little or no rain

marsupial
pouched mammal

▲ Mother and joey

A newborn kangaroo is smaller than your thumb. It stays in its mother's pouch for up to six months, feeding on milk and growing fast. Then the youngster, or joey, hops out for a short while, dashing back if frightened. It finally leaves at one year old.

Kingfishers

One of the world's brightest-coloured birds is shy and quick to hide. It is the Eurasian kingfisher, with its brilliant blue-green and orange-red feathers. There are about 80 kinds of kingfishers around the world, and most are just as brightly coloured. They rarely form flocks and usually nest in holes in riverbanks or trees.

▼▶ Bee-eaters

Just as colourful as kingfishers are their close cousins, the bee-eaters. The 25 kinds live mainly in rainforests in Africa, southern Asia and Australia. They eat bees and wasps, after first knocking off the stings. Carmine bee-eaters breed in groups, in bank or cliff holes.

carmine bee-eater

Word box

migrate
to make a long journey, usually at the time of year when the weather starts to gets cold – many animals travel to warmer places to find food and raise their young.

▶ Rollers

Named after their acrobatic rolling, looping flight, 16 kinds of rollers are found in forests across Africa, southern Asia and Australia. They are close relatives of kingfishers and many have brilliant colouring. They catch flies and other small creatures, in the air and on the ground. Some, such as the lilac-breasted roller, migrate hundreds of kilometres in great flocks.

▼ Eurasian kingfisher

Most kingfishers perch near water, and wait patiently for a fish, frog or perhaps a snake or baby bird. With a flash of colour the kingfisher dives in, spears the prey with its dagger-like beak, and flies away with the meal in its mouth, to its favourite feasting branch.

▼ Ha-ha-ha-ha-ha

One of the biggest, noisiest kingfishers is the kookaburra or 'laughing jackass' of Australia. Its call, to keep other kookaburras away from its territory, sounds like cackling human laughter.

Lions and tigers

Lions and tigers are the largest big cats, strong and stealthy. Lions form groups called prides; tigers usually live alone. Lions like open grassland; tigers prefer thick forests and swamps. A lion is tawny or sandy brown all over; a tiger has black stripes on a yellow or gold background. Both are endangered – especially tigers.

▼ Jungle king?

Lions rarely live in jungles, but the male lion is very kingly. He rarely hunts, but is first to feed. He defends the pride, patrols his region, roars loudly, and leaves signals to show the area is occupied.

▼ Pride life

A pride has up to six females with cubs, plus two or three males who form a friendship known as a coalition. The females care for and feed each other's cubs, and work together to chase and ambush prey as big as zebras.

Wow!
The Siberian tiger is the biggest big cat, 3.5 metres from nose to tail, and 300 kilograms in weight.

▼ Troubled cats

Most lions live in central and southern Africa, with a few in northwest India. There are some very rare tigers, including the large Siberian tiger of east Asia, with just 100 to 200 remaining, and the smaller Sumatran tiger of Southeast Asia, with about 600 left.

Word match

These lion words have got mixed up with their meanings. Can you sort them out?

a. pride   **1.** baby lion
b. cub   **2.** friendly males
c. coalition **3.** group of lions

answers
a3 b1 c2

Siberian tiger

Lizards

Lizards range from tiny geckos to huge monitors as big as crocodiles. They form the largest group of reptiles and most of the 4,500 kinds live in tropical forests. There are also gila monsters in North American deserts, sand skinks in dunes, water-dragons in swamps and house geckos in people's homes. Most eat insects, worms and slugs but some feast on fruits.

Wow!

The slow-worm is not a worm and not always slow — it is a lizard without legs and it can wriggle quite quickly.

▼ Lots of lizards

Monitors are big and strong and catch larger animals such as rats, rabbits, fish, birds and eggs. Like most lizards they have scaly skin, four sprawling legs, four or five sharp-clawed toes on each foot, a long whippy tail, big eyes, and a tongue that flicks out to pick up smells in the air.

▲ Poke out that tongue

When in danger, many lizards hiss, puff themselves up, and perhaps rear up or strike with their claws. Australia's blue-tongued skink also pokes out its bright blue tongue!

the flying lizard of Southeast Asia can extend flaps of skin along its side, to escape enemies by gliding down from a tree

the Nile monitor of Africa eats a range of food, from crabs to carrion, and is an expert swimmer

Gould's goanna from Australia is about 1.5 metres long and is also called the sand monitor

the Komodo dragon of Southeast Asia, the biggest lizard at 3 metres long, can catch wild pigs and deer

Mammals

Find out more:
Bats ◄ Egg-laying mammals ◄
Marsupials ► Rodents ►

The most familiar animals we know – dogs, cats, horses and cows – belong to this group of mammals, and so do we. Mammals are warm-blooded and have babies that feed on their mother's milk. Most are furry or hairy and have four legs and a tail. However, there are plenty of exceptions. Whales and dolphins have almost no hair, and no legs either!

Wow!

Of the 4,450 kinds of mammal, two out of every five are rodents, such as rats and mice. Another one in five is a bat.

► Mammal mothers

All female mammals make milk in their mammary glands to feed their babies. Most mammal mothers, like this baboon mother, also protect their babies and keep them clean and warm.

▲ Strange mammal

The spotted cuscus looks like a monkey. But it is a type of possum – a marsupial from Australia. Like most mammals it has sharp eyes, ears and a keen nose. Its grasping tail can wrap around branches.

Word box

aquatic
living in or suited to water

mammary glands
part of a female mammal's body that makes milk to feed babies

warm-blooded
able to keep body temperature high in any conditions, from hot sun to freezing snow

▼ Fin whale

Mammals move on land, in water and in the air. The second largest mammal is the fin whale, which is 22 metres long and 70 tonnes in weight. Whales are aquatic, with flippers for arms. Semi-aquatic mammals that can get around on land as well as in water include seals, sea lions, otters and water shrews.

◄ Tree shrew

The tree shrew is rather like a small squirrel, with its long, bushy tail. It often builds its nest in trees although some species build their nests at the base of the trunk.

Marsupials

The koala bear is not a real bear, the banded anteater is not a real anteater and the Tasmanian devil is not a real devil. In fact, they are all marsupials. Most mother marsupials have a pouch or pocket of skin on the front of their body. Their tiny babies stay there for weeks, feeding on their mother's milk until they grow strong enough to look after themselves.

▲ Numbat

Many marsupials in Australia are similar to other mammals elsewhere. The numbat, or banded anteater, is a marsupial version of the anteater. There are also marsupial rats, mice and shrews, marsupial moles and marsupial cats, called quolls.

Word box

carnivore
an animal that mainly eats the meat of other animals

scavenge
to search for bits and pieces of left-over food, such as the remains of other animals' meals

▼ Koala

Cuddly-looking koalas live in eucalyptus or gum trees and eat only their leaves. Their close marsupial cousins are wombats, which live in underground tunnels. Other marsupials include kangaroos, wallabies, possums, gliders, bandicoots and bilbies.

▼ Tasmanian devil

The largest marsupial carnivore, the 'devil', has very powerful jaws and teeth, which can even crush bones. It wails and screeches at night, to find a mate or warn other devils to stay away. The female's pouch is a flap of skin and opens 'backwards' towards her tail.

▼ Virginia opossum

Most marsupials live in Australia, some live in Southeast Asia, and a few live in South America. Only the Virginia opossum has spread to North America. It makes its den near people's homes and eats left-over foods.

babies in mother's pouch

Mice and rats

Mice are smaller than rats – otherwise there is little difference between them. All are rodents, with long incisor teeth for nibbling and nipping. Most eat plant foods such as seeds, fruits and roots. They have big eyes and ears, long whiskers and a long tail. They move quickly to escape enemies and breed quickly to keep up their numbers.

mouse

▲ Friendly or harmful?

Mice and rats can be bred and raised as friendly pets. Others are used in scientific research. Wild rats and mice can cause damage to buildings and spread diseases.

Word box

scientific research
experiments that are carried out to find out more about something

sewage
human waste that is carried away in drains

Make some whiskers!

Mice and rats use whiskers to feel in the dark – you can too!

1. Ask an adult to help. Cut a straight line from the edge of a paper plate to its centre. Roll the plate into a cone shape.
2. Stick a few straws onto either side of the cone.
3. Thread some elastic through two tiny holes at the wide end of your cone, to hold the whiskers on your nose.
Now you have your very own mouse whiskers!

▶ Desert-dweller

Like a tiny kangaroo, the jerboa hops at great speed across the sand of the Sahara Desert, using its long tail for balance. Like most rats and mice it hides by day in a burrow and comes out at night to feed.

▲ Country house

The tiny harvest mouse lives in the countryside. Its nest is the size and shape of a tennis ball. The female gives birth to more than ten babies.

Wow!

The house mouse is found in more places around the world than any other animal.

▶ Water-rats

Many rats can swim well. A water-rat is often just a brown rat searching for fish or crabs (or gobbling up sewage). The Australian water rat is a large rat, with a head and body 35 centimetres long. It dives well and eats frogs, fish, lizards, snakes, other rats and mice, waterbirds and even fish-catching bats.

Australian water rat

Microscopic creatures

Find out more:
Crabs and other crustaceans ◄

There are millions of creatures all around us that we cannot see – they are too small. We need a microscope to view this tiny world. Some of these micro-living things are true animals, but very small. Others are made of just one living unit or 'cell' each, and they often have both animal and plant features. These are not true animals. They are known as protists.

Wow!

After tardigrades have been dried out, they can be brought back to life by adding water – even 50 years later.

▲ Water-bears

Big tardigrades or water-bears are just about large enough for us to see, with their tubby bodies and stubby limbs. They live in water and damp places like moss. These animals can survive being dried out, frozen or almost boiled.

▶ Amoeba

Like most protists, the amoeba lives in water. It is a single cell, flexible and baglike, and oozes along in pond mud. It catches even smaller living things, such as bacteria, by extending bloblike 'arms' around them or simply flowing over them.

▼ Round animals

The rotifer has a circle of micro-hairs around its mouth end, like a crown. The hairs wave and filter any edible bits from the water and pass them into its vase-shaped body. This tiny creature is also called the 'wheel-animacule'.

▼ Swarming seas

A drop of sea water contains thousands of tiny living things. Heliozoans are protists with a central shell-like chamber made of silica. Their long, thin, starlike 'arms' catch even smaller prey. Foraminiferan protists look like micro-snails and also have a hard-shelled central part with flexible tentacles.

▲ Shrimp cousins

Copepods are tiny cousins of shrimps and crabs. They swim by waving their very long antennae (feelers), and swarm in their billions. Their bristly front limbs filter food particles from sea water. Copepods are food for bigger ocean animals such as baby fish.

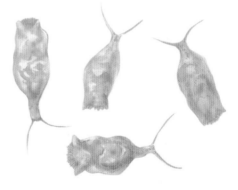

Word box

cell
a self-contained unit of life – a protist is just one cell

silica
a natural substance or mineral that forms sand, glass, and the shells of some living things

tentacle
a long, slim, bendy body part

Migrating animals

Find out more:
Antarctic animals ◄ Butterflies and moths ◄
Turtles and tortoises ► Whales ►

Every spring in Europe, swallows and swifts appear like magic, and in North America, monarch butterflies do the same. These are migrants. They make long journeys, usually to the same place and back again each year. They go to the best place for finding food or raising their young, usually somewhere warmer.

► Birds

Birds migrate further than any other animal. Many kinds, from geese to buntings, leave Europe, central Asia and North America in spring for the Arctic summer, then return south in autumn. Swallows spend the winter in Africa and come to Europe for the summer.

grey whale migration route

Wow!

The Arctic tern travels further than any other bird. It has two summers each year, in the Arctic and Antarctic — a return trip of 30,000 kilometres.

▼ Reptiles

Sea turtles, such as green turtles, are wandering migrants that roam the oceans. Every two or three years they may swim about 1,000 kilometres to the beaches where they hatched, to lay their own eggs.

▲ Mammals

Many great whales, such as greys, swim from warm tropical waters to the far north or south, for the brief summer when food is plentiful.

Word box

roost
a resting or sleeping place, usually for flying animals such as birds, bats and insects

tundra
treeless land around the Arctic Ocean, with low bushes and mossy bogs, covered in winter snow

◄ Insects

Monarch butterflies spend the winter crowded in roosts in south-west North America. In spring they head north to Canada, breeding as they go. Their 'grandchild' butterflies come back in autumn.

Monkeys

Most monkeys are bright-eyed, long-tailed, clever, day-active tree-dwellers with grasping hands and feet. They live in troops, communicate with noisy whoops and chattering, and eat plant foods such as flowers, fruits, berries and shoots. There are 240 different kinds of monkeys, with different lifestyles and habitats.

▼ White-cheeked

Over 20 kinds of small monkeys live in Central and South America. Many have long, silky fur, and claws rather than fingernails and toenails. Manabeys sleep and spend nearly all their time in the trees. Troops of about 10 to 30 live together and are extremely noisy, constantly chattering across the treetops.

white-cheeked
mangabey

Word scramble

Unscramble these words to find the names of five types of monkeys:

a. EQUACAM
b. LIRDNALM
c. RELSQURI YEKNOM
d. REDISP YEKNOM
e. BUSCOLO

answers
a. macaque b. mandrill
c. squirrel monkey
d. spider monkey e. colobus

▲ Vervets

Vervets range widely across Africa. They climb well, run fast and swim rapidly. They live in grassland, scrub and forest. Vervets eat plants, small animals and insects.

▶ Howler monkey

Howler monkeys are large monkeys that live in South America. They eat mainly fruits and leaves. The howler monkey is named after its very loud call.

▶ Ring-tailed lemurs

Monkeys are in the primate group of mammals, along with apes and prosimians – 80 kinds of lemurs, bushbabies, pottos, lorises and tarsiers. These are mostly small tree-dwellers. Lemurs, such as this ring-tailed lemur, are found only on Madagascar, an island east of Africa.

Mountain animals

Find out more:
Butterflies and moths ◄ Cats ◄
Eagles and hawks ◄ Rodents ►

Mountains are harsh, dangerous places, as snowstorms howl across icy cliffs. Yet some animals are specialized to survive here. Mountain creatures need warm coverings of thick fur or feathers, and feet with strong grips for slippery rocks. Many larger animals migrate or journey higher in summer, as the ice melts and plants grow in alpine meadows. They travel back down to the sheltered lower forests for winter.

▼ Lammergeier

Great birds of prey seek old, sick or injured animals to eat. The lammergeier, a vulture of Europe, Africa and Asia, takes an animal bone up high. It drops it onto a rock, to break open and reveal the soft marrow inside.

▲ Mountain lion

The mountain lion, also called the puma or cougar, is not a real lion – but is a similar colour. It once thrived in many habitats throughout the Americas. But hunting by people drove it to remote mountains. This cat eats a variety of prey, from rabbits to mountain goats, sheep and deer.

▼ Chilly chinchilla

Many mountain animals have become rare, killed for the thick fur that keeps them warm on the cold heights. The chinchilla, a plant-eating rodent of the Andes Mountains, in South America, is still rare in the wild. But it is also bred for its fur, and as a soft, cuddly pet.

▲ Apollo butterfly

The apollo of Europe and Asia can flap strongly in the wind to fly at over 3,000 metres – higher than almost any butterfly. It feeds on nectar from alpine flowers. Most mountain insects survive winter as eggs, or hide in cracks in rocks.

Word box

alpine
to do with mountains – Alpine with a capital 'A' is to do with the Alps range of mountains in Europe

marrow
soft, jelly-like substance inside many types of bones

remote
distant

Nests

Find out more:
Animal societies ◀ Birds ◀ Eagles and hawks ◀
Hibernating animals ◀ Sea birds ▶

Our homes are, in a way, our nests. A nest is a place where a creature can safely rest and raise its young. It is usually comfortable, lined with grass, moss, hairs, leaves or feathers. Birds are well-known nesters. Some build nests from twigs. Others peck a hole in a tree or steal another animal's burrow. Many other animals make nests too, from ants to alligators.

bubbles

cichlids

▲ Bubble-nesting fish

Some fish make nests of mud, twigs, pebbles – or bubbles. Certain gouramis and cichlids 'blow' long-lasting bubbles with a foamy liquid. The bubbles collect under a leaf or among stems. The female lays her eggs there and the male protects them until the baby fish develop.

▲ Wasp nest

Insects that make nests include bees, wasps, ants and termites. Wasps make a papery substance by chewing wood with their saliva (spit), and build their nest with it.

Wow!

The biggest mammal nests, made in bushes by wild pigs and hogs, are 3 metres across, with bent-over branches forming a roof.

▲ Food delivery

Many birds use natural holes rather than building a nest. The colourful hoopoe of Europe, Africa and Asia nests in a hole or opening in a bank, wall, tree or even a building. The female sits on her eggs to keep them warm and safe for about 18 days, and the male brings her food.

Octopuses and squid

Find out more:
Deep sea animals ◀ Sea animals ▶
Shellfish ▶ Snails and slugs ▶

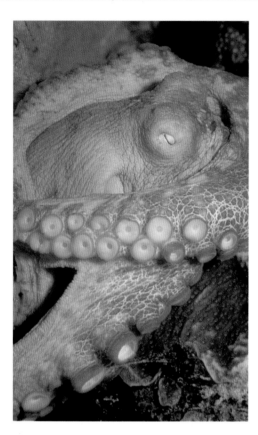

The squid belongs to the animal group called molluscs or 'shellfish'. The squid has a shell, but it is small and flat, inside the body. Its close cousins are octopuses, cuttlefish and nautiluses. They all have big eyes, squishy bodies and long, flexible tentacles with suckers for grabbing their prey. These animals are all fierce predators.

◀ Lurking in a lair

The octopus's eight tentacles join its body around its beaklike mouth. By day it lurks in a sea-bed cave or among rocks. At night it catches crabs, fish and other victims. In captivity, an octopus can recognize shapes and colours and learn tricks.

Word box

captivity
when an animal is kept and looked after by humans

siphon
in molluscs, a bendy tube on the side of the body, through which water can be sucked in or squirted out

▼ Hidden arms

The cuttlefish's two long 'arms' are usually hidden under its eight tentacles. They shoot out to grab crabs, small fish, shellfish and worms. Cuttlefish can change their colour more, and faster, than any other animal – from almost white to nearly black in a second.

Wow!

The giant squid is the largest invertebrate (animal without a backbone) – it has a total length of more than 20 metres.

▶ Squid

The giant squid is a huge deep-sea predator, with eight tentacles and two longer sucker-tipped 'arms'. Like octopuses, squid swim by taking in water and squirting it out as a powerful jet through their siphon.

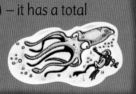

▲ Twilight hunter

The nautilus's curly shell is mostly filled with gas, to help it float in mid-water. The animal itself takes up only the wide opening. It hunts fish and other prey, using its huge eyes to see in the dim depths.

No other bird looks quite like an owl.
There are about 200 kinds. These birds hunt prey in darkness using their huge eyes and amazingly good hearing. They catch it with their large, strong toes tipped with sharp talons. By day, most owls rest on a branch or in a hollow tree, cave or quiet building.

◀ Tawny owl

Most medium-sized owls, such as the tawny, hunt mice, rats, baby rabbits, insects such as large beetles and grasshoppers, and perhaps small birds and bats. As it rests on a tree branch by day, its patterned brown plumage makes it very difficult to see.

◀ Spotted eagle owl

Eagle owls are among the biggest owls, with wings spanning 150 centimetres. They mainly catch other birds as they sleep, including pigeons, blackbirds and thrushes. Bats and other owls, such as tawnies, are also their prey, and they even snatch baby eagles or hawks from their nests.

Wow!

The barn owl lives almost everywhere except icy Antarctica — no other land bird is so widespread.

Word scramble

Unscramble these words to find the names of five types of owls:

a. NOWYS
b. NYWAT
c. NOGL-REDEA
d. SHROT-RAEDE
e. RINGOWRUB

answers
a. snowy b. tawny c. long-eared d. short-eared e. burrowing

▶ Barn owl

The ghostly-white barn owl once roosted and nested in hollow trees or caves, but barns, churches and outbuildings do just as well. Like other owls it has a wide, round, bowl-shaped face. Its feathers have very soft edges so they make almost no sound as the owl flies and swoops.

Parrots

Noisy, colourful and clever – parrots are popular as pets. But capturing them from the wild means some of the 350 kinds are now very rare. The parrot group also includes parakeets, lorikeets (lories), cockatoos, rosellas and macaws. Most live in tropical forests and eat fruits, seeds, nuts and other plant parts. Smaller types such as budgerigars and lovebirds thrive in captivity.

► Rainbow lorikeet

Like most parrots in flocks, rainbow lories are noisy, with endless flapping and squawking. Nicknamed 'painting-by-numbers' birds, from their bright patches of plumage, lories are bold. In Australia and the West Pacific islands they can be seen in parks and gardens.

Wow!

Budgies (budgerigars) are bred in all colours, from red and blue to yellow, white and grey. All wild budgies that live in Australia are green.

▲ Scarlet macaw

This huge macaw cracks nuts with its powerful beak. Female and male stay together, even flying with wings almost touching. They may form larger family flocks of about 20, in woods and on farms across Central and South America.

► White cockatoo

This is one of several parrots that can learn tricks such as counting. Many parrots also 'talk' by copying human voices – but they don't understand what they are saying!

▲ Parrot

Parrots are brilliantly coloured birds that chatter loudly as they fly around the rainforest. Their bills are specially shaped for eating nuts.

Pests

Find out more:
Birds ◄ Desert animals ◄ Flies ◄
Insects ◄ Mice and rats ◄

Word box

diseases
illnesses that are caught
and can be quite serious

swarm
a huge gathering of insects or
similar small animals

It is a picnic on a sunny day. A wasp hovers near the jam, a fly lands on the food, the apple has a huge maggot in it, and the bread has been nibbled by a mouse! Animal pests are everywhere. Some eat or spoil our foods, either as crops growing in fields, or stored in warehouses or cupboards. Other pests spread germs and diseases. There are even pests, such as woodworms and termites, which eat through furniture and wooden houses.

▲ Locusts

In some years, locusts breed to form gigantic swarms. They darken the sky like storm clouds, and destroy whole farms. 'Locust-watcher' workers report their build-up, so they can be sprayed with poison before the swarm grows too big.

▲ Red-billed quelea

This African seed-eater, a type of weaverbird, is sometimes called the 'feathered locust'. It forms huge flocks that land on farms and eat wheat, rice and similar crops. Guns, nets, traps and poisons have been tried against the quelea, but it is still a major pest.

▼ Pesky rats!

Brown, black and rice rats, and house mice, can be great pests. They ruin stores of food by leaving urine and droppings in them. They also gnaw electrical wires. The fleas that live on black rats can spread diseases.

black rat

◄ Tiny but deadly

Flies are perhaps the most deadly animals in the world, because they spread the germs that cause diseases. Houseflies enter homes and infect food. Mosquitoes like this one carry malaria and yellow fever, blackflies carry river-blindness and testse flies spread sleeping-sickness.

Some of our best friends are animals – dogs, cats, gerbils, hamsters and budgies. Pets are animals we look after, and they provide interest and fun. Some people keep unusual pets such as snakes or lizards, or even tarantulas! Various kinds of pets are popular in different parts of the world, such as monkeys in Asia, parrots in South America, possums in Australia, raccoons in North America and mongooses in Africa.

◄ Big pet

A pony needs lots of space, time, food and care. It can give rides or pull a cart. Like many pets, it can be taken to shows and maybe win prizes!

zebra fish

◄ Best friend

Dogs can be marvellous pets, but sometimes they have a hard time. They may not be taken for enough walks. They try to behave well, but their owners may teach them badly, and then shout at them. With time and thought from a caring owner, a dog's life can be very happy.

bulldog

◄ Fish

Fish in an aquarium or tank depend completely on their owner. They need to be fed daily. The tank must be regularly topped up with water – and cleaned out.

▼ Suitable pet

Hamsters are small, quiet, and happy in a large cage with plenty of toys, tunnels and rooms. They suit people who have little space.

► Pet needs

Cats can look after themselves and be left alone more than dogs. But like any pet, they have needs – fresh water, healthy food and cleaning out when necessary. Cats need a quiet place to rest and sleep, and, like other cuddly pets, a friendly stroke.

Poisonous animals

Find out more:
Frogs and toads ◄ Insects ◄
Shellfish ► Snakes ► Spiders ►

Several kinds of animals are poisonous to people. Some are truly deadly. But their venoms are not designed to kill us. The animal uses its poisonous bite or sting to catch its prey, or to defend itself against enemies. There are various kinds of poisonous snakes, fish, scorpions and insects, as well as the blue-ringed octopus, snail-like animals called cone shells, and stinging jellyfish.

Wow!

Australia has more poisonous animals, for its size, than any other country — including eight of the world's ten deadliest snakes.

arrow-poison
frogs

▼ Ready to strike

Cobras have large fangs that inject strong poison. Like most other creatures, they bite only if cornered, trapped or surprised. The poison is really meant for prey. The king cobra is the biggest poisonous snake, at 5 metres long, and its victims are other snakes.

cobra

▲ Warning!

The bright colours of arrow-poison frogs and lionfish (dragonfish) are a warning: leave me alone! The poison is in the frog's skin and the fish's fin spines. Any animal that tries to eat them becomes very ill, and learns to avoid bright colours.

lionfish

▼ Similar colours

Several very different kinds of animals are yellow and black or red and black in colour, to warn others about their stings, poisonous flesh or skin. They include bees, wasps like this hornet, beetles such as ladybirds, butterflies, frogs, toads, snakes and salamanders.

▼ Desert scorpion

The scorpion's tail-tip is poisonous. When the scorpion feels threatened, it arches its tail over its head. It might use the sting to quieten a struggling victim like a mouse. Otherwise, it is used for self-defence.

Word box

fang
a large, sharp tooth

venom
another name for poison

Find out more:
Arctic animals ◄ Camouflage ◄ Mammals ◄

Rabbits and hares have long back legs, long ears, a 'bob' tail, quivering nose and big eyes alert for danger. They are all plant-eaters, and most dig underground homes called warrens. Although they look similar to rodents (gnawing animals), rabbits and hares have their own mammal group with 80 kinds worldwide.

▼ Common hare

A hare is like a large rabbit, with very long ears and legs. Hares live in open fields and hide from danger among the grasses. They are often active at night, when they nibble plants. Young hares are born with fur and their eyes wide open.

Word box

'bob' tail
a short, rounded or fluffy tail

moult
when an animal's fur, feathers or skin loosens and comes off, as a new layer grows beneath

warren
a rabbit family's home of burrows and chambers

◄▲ New coat

The snowshoe hare moults twice a year. In summer it is brown, to blend in with soil and dry grass. In winter it is white, to merge with the snow. Its camouflage makes it hard for predators, such as wolves and lynx, to spot it.

► Rabbit cousin

The rabbit group includes short-eared, short-legged members called pikas. Like rabbits, they eat grass and seeds. They live in family groups in burrows, in Asia and North America. Pikas store food in their burrows to eat in winter.

Wow!

Hares are some of the fastest runners, leaping along at more than 70 kilometres an hour.

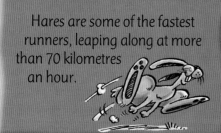

◄ Whistling rabbit

Found only in a few mountainous places in Mexico, the small volcano rabbit has short ears and legs. It is noisy too! Most rabbits and hares thump the ground to warn of danger. The volcano rabbit whistles loudly to its family group.

Reptiles

Find out more:
Crocodiles and alligators ◀ Lizards ◀
Snakes ▶ Turtles and tortoises ▶

Reptiles are the animals some people 'love to hate'. They include slithering snakes, sneaky lizards, lurking crocodiles and angry alligators. But they are varied and fascinating creatures, with almost 8,000 kinds in all habitats, from mountaintops to the open sea. Reptiles are cold-blooded, have scaly skin, and most lay eggs. The main groups are snakes, lizards, turtles and tortoises, and crocodiles and alligators.

gharial

▲ Slim mouth

Crocodiles and alligators make up the smallest reptile group, but are biggest in body size. They have large, lumpy plates of bone in their scaly skin, especially along their backs. The gharial (gavial) is a 7-metre-long crocodile from southern Asia, with long, narrow jaws. It spends much time in water, hunting fish.

Wow!

The legless reptiles called worm-lizards are not worms, or lizards, but a soil-living combination of lizard and snake – and very fierce hunters of real worms.

Reptiles – true or false?

1. all reptiles lay eggs
2. all reptiles have legs
3. all reptiles are cold-blooded
4. all reptiles have scales

4. false, but only just – a few reptiles have leathery skin
3. true – reptiles cannot keep their bodies warm all the time, like mammals and birds can
2. false – snakes, worm-lizards and some lizards have no legs
1. false – some snakes and lizards give birth to babies

◀ Frilly neck

The frilled lizard of Australian woods spreads out the large, colourful flap of skin around its neck to look bigger and more frightening to its enemies. It also opens its mouth wide, hisses and jumps about. If that fails, it rears up on its back legs and runs away! Lizards form the biggest group of reptiles.

▶ Dinosaur survivor

The tuatara is the only surviving member of a reptile group that thrived at the time of the dinosaurs. It lives on a few New Zealand islands, eats small creatures, and can live to be 100!

Rhinos and tapirs

Rhinos are the most threatened big animals in the world. There are only five kinds left. The white (square-lipped) rhino numbers several thousand. But the black (hook-lipped) rhino, also of Africa, and the Indian, Sumatran and Javan rhinos of Asia are in desperate trouble. These massive plant-eaters have lost their natural habitats and are killed for their horns.

Word box

horn
a long, sharp-pointed animal part, and also the substance from which scales and claws are made

◄▼ African rhinos

Most rhinos live alone, except for a mother with her calf (baby), or a male and female at mating time. In Africa the black rhino (seen below), which is really grey, eats leaves from bushes and herbs. The white one (left), (which is also grey, or sometimes yellow-brown), prefers grasses.

▼ Rhino cousin

Tapirs are piglike animals from the forests of Southeast Asia, and Central and South America. Like rhinos, most have three hoofed toes on each foot. Tapirs love water and swim well. They sniff out plant food using their trunklike noses.

Wow!
The white rhino is the largest land animal after elephants — it is almost 5 metres long including its tail, and weighs more than 2 tonnes.

▼ Indian rhino

The rhino's horn is horn-shaped, but not made of the animal substance horn. It is made of hairs squeezed and stuck together in a hard mass, which grows in a horn shape.

River and lake animals

Find out more:
Beavers ◀ Crocodiles and alligators ◀
Fish ◀ Rodents ▶

We see only shadowy shapes near the surface.
Yet rivers, lakes, streams, ponds and other fresh water
habitats teem with animal life. In small puddles there are
tiny worms and water-fleas that would easily fit into this
'o'. Then there are aquatic insects, snails, thousands of
kinds of fish, frogs and snakes, waterbirds and otters.
The largest water animals are giant hippos and crocodiles.

▲ Deadly teeth

Piranhas eat all kinds of foods,
from seeds to worms. If a large
animal in the water struggles or
bleeds, dozens of piranhas gather
in a 'feeding frenzy' and bite lumps
off it. In a minute or two they strip
its flesh, leaving just the bones.

Word box

freshwater
made of non-salty water

graze
to eat grasses and other
low-growing plants

rodent
gnawing mammal, like a rat

Word scramble

Unscramble these words to find
the names of five types of river
and pond animals:

a. SHIFERGINK (bird)
b. RATEW WERSH (mammal)
c. ERGEN GROF (amphibian)
d. GIVNID ELEBET (insect)
e. SHERFRATEW SELSUM
(shellfish)

answers
a. kingfisher b. water shrew
c. green frog d. diving beetle
e. freshwater mussel

▶ Huge gnawer

The capybara of South America
is the largest rodent. It weighs
60 kilograms – as much as an adult
person. It lives in family groups around
swamps and lakes. To escape its main
enemy on land, the jaguar, it dives into the
water. But it may be snapped up by
a crocodile-like caiman.

▼ Lightweight trotter

Jacanas or lilytrotters have very
long toes, angled out wide to
spread their weight, so they really
can walk on lily pads. Like many
waterbirds they swim well. They eat
a mix of small animals and plants.

◀ Grazing giant

Hippos wallow in African rivers
and lakes by day, then graze on
nearby grasslands at night. Males
fight in water with their huge, tusk-
like teeth to claim their territory,
so they can mate with females.

Rodents

Find out more:
Beavers ◄ Mammals ◄ Mice and rats ◄ Pests ◄
Squirrels ►

Gnaw, gnash, nibble, nip – rodents are all mammals with long incisor teeth. They use their teeth for many purposes – cracking open nuts and seeds, scraping bark, cutting through wood, digging in soil and biting in self-defence. With 1,700 types of rodents worldwide, they form the largest mammal group. Rodents include rats, mice, voles, lemmings, hamsters, gerbils, squirrels, gophers, beavers, porcupines and guinea pigs.

Word box

cavies
rodent group from South America, which includes guinea pigs, chinchillas, and the huge capybaras

► Cute chipmunk

The familiar North American chipmunk is a type of squirrel. It visits picnic areas, parks and gardens for leftover foods, and is sometimes kept as a pet. It stores seeds, nuts and berries in its burrow to eat during the winter.

▼ Coypu cavy

At 1 metre from its nose to its tail, the coypu is like a huge rat. It belongs to the rodent group called cavies. Coypus swim well with their webbed feet, dig burrows in banks and eat water plants.

Wow!

A porcupine cannot shoot out its spines like arrows, but it can jab them into an enemy – and they are very painful to pull out!

▲ Gobbling gopher

Gophers are squirrels that live mostly underground and alone, like moles. They dig tunnels with their paws and teeth, and feed on roots, bulbs and other underground plant parts. Sometimes their burrows and eating habits damage farm crops.

◄ Prickly porcupine

Porcupines are plant-eaters. There are about 20 different kinds, which are all active at night. They have long, sharp spines that are really extra-thick hairs.

Sea animals

Find out more:
Deep sea animals ◀ Dolphins ◀ Fish ◀
Seals and sea lions ▶ Sharks ▶

The sea is the world's biggest habitat. It extends from rocky coasts, the shallows of coral reefs, and the icebergs of the polar regions. The vast open ocean stretches over most of the Earth and plumbs the darkest depths. Apart from insects, all kinds of animals live in the sea. Scientists are still discovering new kinds of creatures in bays, undersea caves and canyons.

▼ Snakes at sea?

Sea snakes are not just ordinary snakes out for a swim. They are fully suited to ocean life, with a flattened, paddle-like tail, for swimming. Sea snakes are cousins of cobras and just as poisonous, killing fish for food.

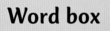

Word box

canyon
a deep, narrow, steep-sided valley

food chain
series of stages where a plant is eaten by an animal, and that animal is eaten by another, and so on

plankton
tiny plants and animals drifting in water

▲ Millions of fish

Small fish move around in vast shoals of many millions. They are important links in the sea food chains. They feed on tiny plants and animals in the plankton, then they become meals for bigger fish and other sea predators.

◀ 'Cow' of the sea

Manatees or dugongs live in tropical waters. They stay near the shore and eat sea-grasses and other plants, giving these animals the nickname of 'sea-cows'.

◀ Not what they seem

Sea creatures are often unfamiliar and puzzling. Jellyfish may look like floppy flowers, but they are proper animals — in fact they are deadly predators. Their trailing tentacles sting and capture prey, such as small fish.

Sea birds

Sea birds depend on the sea for their food. Sea birds include huge albatrosses, smaller petrels and prions, tropic-birds, frigate-birds, gannets, boobies, gulls and auks. Most have long, slim wings for soaring, webbed feet for swimming and catch fish and squid from near the water's surface.

Wow!

The wandering albatross has the longest wings of any bird — more than 3 metres from tip to tip.

▲ Dive of death

The gannet plunge-dives like an arrow from 30 metres up in the air and seizes its unsuspecting prey in its dagger-like bill.

▼ A place to breed

Most sea birds breed along cliffs and rocky shores. Puffins lay their eggs in burrows, which they build themselves or have taken over from rabbits or other birds.

Word box

incubate
to keep something warm so it develops properly, like a bird sitting on its egg

krill
small shrimplike creatures of the ocean

▲ Amazing albatross

An albatross glides for days without flapping, gaining height by heading into the wind. It swoops down to snatch food from the sea and touches land only to breed.

▲ Storm petrel

True to its name, the tiny storm petrel flies in the worst storms and gales. It skims over the sea, looking for food such as krill and baby fish. Some petrels form vast flocks of many millions of birds.

Seals and sea lions

Is the sea lion a 'lion-of-the-sea'? Yes, sort of. It is a fast, fierce and hungry hunter of fish, sea birds, shellfish and other creatures. In fact, a big sea lion is huge, weighing more than a tonne – four times as much as a real lion! All 35 kinds of sea lions and seals are speedy hunters. They live mainly along coasts, coming onto land only to rest and breed.

◄ Seal or sea lion?

Seals have no ear flaps. They wriggle on land and swim with their back flippers. This Australian sea lion has tiny ear flaps. It props itself up on its front flippers, tucking the back flippers under to waddle on land. It swims with its front flippers.

▲ On the rocks

Most seals and sea lions, like this northern fur seal, breed in groups on beaches or rocky shores. The pups (babies) soon have to learn to swim and survive on their own.

▲ Tusks

The Arctic walrus uses its tusks to pull shellfish from the sea bed – and to show off to other walruses at breeding time. Like many seals and sea lions, the walrus can dive deep under the water and stay there for over half an hour.

Make seal flippers

1. Swish your hand through a bowl of water with your fingers spread wide.

2. Now, put a plastic bag over your hand. Your hand is now like a seal flipper. Swish your hand through the water again – see how much more water a seal can push with its flipper.

A seal's flippers help it to swim faster!

Wow!

The male elephant seal can be so fat that he weighs as much as a real elephant – almost 5 tonnes!

► A cold baby?

No. Seals and sea lions have thick fur coats and also a layer of fat under their skin, called blubber. This keeps them warm, even when lying on ice! The young harp seal of the North Atlantic loses its snowy-white coat after a few weeks, and grows dark, waterproof fur.

Seashore animals

Find out more:
Crabs and other crustaceans ◄ Fish ◄
Sea birds ◄

A day at the seaside can be fun, but imagine a lifetime there – day and night in the wind, rain and snow. Imagine the storms with crashing waves and rolling boulders. The seashore is a tough habitat! Most animals hide in sand or mud, or under rocks or seaweed. As the tide comes in, they come out to feed and breed.

▼ Shorebirds

Many birds live near the shore including these gulls, and waders like oystercatchers. They like the 'strand line', where the tide leaves bits and pieces behind as it goes back out.

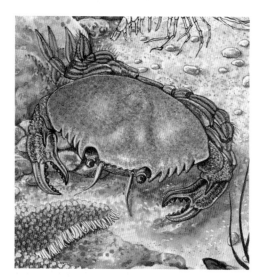

◄ Shore crab

The shore crab is found in many parts of the world – even in deep water and estuaries. It eats almost any kind of food, including rotting fish and slimy seaweeds.

▼ Goby

Gobies are bottom-dwelling fish, often found in shallow waters. Some bury themselves in mud.

Wow!

The boot-lace worm of the shore is hardly thicker than a real boot-lace – yet it is one of the world's longest animals at over 20 metres!

▼ Sea anemones

These simple animals are cousins of jellyfish and corals. Their tentacles grab and sting prey like shrimps and fish. When the tentacles are pulled inwards, the anemone looks like a blob of jelly.

Word scramble

Unscramble these words to find the names of four types of small, simple seashore animals:

a. ROLAC
b. GENSOP
c. ENOMANE
d. GARMORW

answers
a. coral b. sponge
c. anemone d. ragworm

Sharks

There are 330 kinds of shark and they are all meat-eaters. Some sharks filter prey from the water, or lie in wait for victims on the sea bed, rather than speeding through the open ocean after them. Although most fish are bony, the skeleton of a shark is made of cartilage. This is lighter and more elastic than bone.

◀ Hammerhead

Like all sharks, this 6-metre hunter has an amazing sense of smell and can detect blood in the water from many kilometres away. A shark's skin is like sandpaper, because its scales are shaped like tiny versions of the sharp teeth in its mouth. Most sharks live alone, but hammerheads gather together in groups to breed.

▼ Stingray

Rays are close cousins of sharks. Most glide across the sea bed on their wide 'wings', searching for buried shellfish and worms, which they crush with their wide, flat-topped teeth. The stingray's poison sting is like a dagger blade halfway along its tail.

sting

Wow!

The whale shark is the world's biggest fish, 13 metres long and 15 tonnes in weight — yet it eats only tiny creatures such as krill and baby fish.

▼ Super-hunter

The great white shark is the biggest meat-eating fish, at 7 metres long. It eats whatever it likes! Other fish, seals, sea birds, sea turtles, small dolphins and giant whales are all its victims. The smallest members of the shark group include dogfish, which are less than 60 centimetres long.

great white shark

Shellfish

Find out more:
Crabs and other crustaceans ◄ Octopuses and squid ◄
Sea animals ◄ Seashore animals ◄ Snails and slugs ►

Shellfish have shells, but they are not fish. Most belong to the animal group called molluscs, cousins of slugs and snails. Many live along the seashore, on rocks or in sand and mud. Their shells protect against the hot sun, drying wind, pounding waves and their enemies. Crabs, lobsters and shrimps are also sometimes called shellfish, although they are crustaceans, not molluscs.

mussels

▲ Strong mussels

Mussels, oysters, cockles, clams and similar shellfish take in sea water and filter tiny bits of food from it. Mussels attach themselves to rocks with strong threads, as though tied by string.

Word scramble

Unscramble these words to find the names of five types of shellfish:

a. KHELW
b. SLACLOP
c. ZELLORARSH
d. LEKCOC
e. LEKWIN

answers
a. whelk b. scallop
c. razorshell d. cockle
e. winkle

▼ A lucky find

Some oysters contain beautiful shiny pearls, used for jewellery. The oyster makes the pearl around a bit of stone or grit that falls into its shell, which it cannot remove.

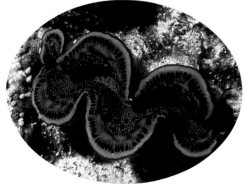

▲ Big blue lips

The giant clam is the biggest shellfish, and can be 1 metre across. Its fleshy, frilly 'lips' help it to breathe under the water and to see! Shellfish have no proper head and no ears or nose. But they have lots of tiny 'eyes' that can detect patches of light and dark and shadows.

▲ Cone shell

Cone shells really do have cone-shaped shells. This is the West African garter cone, a typical example with its decorated shell. It can grow to 7 centimetres long.

Wow!

Cone shells have a very poisonous 'bite' that can even kill a person!

Snails and slugs

Find out more:
Octopuses and squid ◄ Seashore animals ◄
Shellfish ◄

They move so slowly, it is amazing they survive at all. Slugs and snails thrive in woods, ponds, rivers, even dry grasslands and deserts. A snail has a curly shell for protection, but most slugs do not – except for shelled slugs! Slugs and snails are both molluscs, and there over 50,000 kinds worldwide.

flavescene slug

▲ Nudibranch

The name of this sea slug means 'naked gill'. Nudibranchs don't have a shell to protect their gills. They are poisonous and brightly coloured to warn predators to keep away.

Word box

mucus
a slimy, slippery, sticky substance made by animals (and by us in our noses)

predators
animals that hunt and eat other animals

Wow!

Some types of snail are male or female, some types change from one to the other as they grow, and some are male and female at the same time!

▼ Moving house

The snail's shell protects its body. The head has two tentacles, tipped with simple eyes that detect shadows and light areas. There is a mouth on the underside.

◄ Sliming along

Slugs and snails use plenty of mucus to slide along. The mucus puts off attackers who may want to eat them. Slugs and snails like damp places best and prefer to come out after rain or at night.

giant snail

Snakes

It is hard to mistake a snake – it has no legs.
Because snakes are hunters they have long teeth for
grabbing prey. But these reptiles cannot chew – they must
swallow food whole. There are almost 3,000 kinds of
snakes, and apart from the icy polar regions, they live
all over the world – even in the open ocean. Less than
30 types of snakes are truly deadly to people.

▼ Poisonous fangs

Poisonous snakes, such as this cobra, use their venom to kill or
quieten prey, so it cannot run away or struggle while being
swallowed. Cobras, kraits, mambas and coral-snakes have their
poison-jabbing fangs near the front of the mouth. The fangs of
vipers, sidewinders, adders
and rattlesnakes are hinged to
fold back when not being used.

Wow!

The longest snakes are royal
pythons, which grow up to 10 metres
long. They could
wrap around you
12 times!

▲ A big hug

Pythons and boas, like this
Madagascan tree boa, are mostly
big, heavy snakes. They can wrap
around prey so it cannot breathe.
Big pythons and boas can swallow
prey as large as wild pigs and small
antelopes – including the horns!

Word box

pits
holes

vibrations
shaking movements

▶ See, hear, smell and taste

The Aruba rattlesnake shows how sensitive snakes
are. It sees quite well, especially movements. It hears
well too, and feels vibrations in the ground. The tongue flicks
out to smell and 'taste' the air. Rattlesnakes are pit-vipers and
have pits under the eyes. These detect heat, so the snake can catch
a warm-blooded victim like a mouse even in complete darkness.

Spiders

A spider has eight legs, unlike insects, which have six legs. Nearly all spiders have a poisonous bite, using their fanglike mouthparts, but only a few are harmful to people. Most spin silk from their rear ends to make webs for catching small prey, such as flies.

tarantula

▲ Big and hairy

Tarantulas and bird-eating spiders are big, strong and hairy, and live in the tropics, mainly in the Americas. They hunt at night for small animals such as mice, shrews and baby birds.

▼ On the prowl

Some spiders do not use webs for catching prey. They simply chase, overpower and bite their prey. The wolf spider is one of these. Like most spiders, it has eight eyes — and these are large, so it can follow its victim.

▲ Funnelweb

The funnelweb of Australia has strong fangs and powerful poison. It is dangerous because it lives in or near people's homes. It rears up and strikes quickly, unlike most spiders, which usually run away.

Wow!

A web-spinning spider makes a new web almost every night — eating the old one to recycle (use again) the silk threads.

◀ House spider

The house spider spins an untidy web in a corner, and eats most small creatures that blunder into it. Spiders do not really like baths — they tend to slip in and cannot crawl out.

Squirrels

Squirrels have bright eyes, a bushy tail and sharp claws. A typical squirrel leaps through trees, nibbles seeds and buries nuts. Some squirrels prefer flowers or fruits to nuts. Some glide on flaps of furry skin that lie along the sides of the body. Others have small, stumpy tails and never climb trees. The 250 types of squirrel are all rodent mammals, cousins of beavers, rats and mice.

▼ At home with the prairie dogs

Named after their doglike 'yips', prairie dogs are ground squirrels of North American grasslands. They dig complicated burrows with many entrances and chambers as a home for one male, several females and their young. The burrow entrance has soil piled around it to keep out water during floods. Many similar burrows over a wide area are called a township.

Word box

hibernate
to sleep very deeply for weeks, usually to survive a long winter

prairie
grasslands or the wide-open plains of North America

▲ Grey squirrel

The grey squirrel of North America easily leaps wide distances among the branches of trees, using its tail to balance and steer.

▲ Arctic ground squirrel

This ground squirrel is also called a marmot. It lives in a burrow and eats a wide variety of grasses, seeds, buds and shoots. Like many squirrels in places that have cold winters, it hibernates in its burrow for several months.

▼

Starfish and urchins

Find out more:
Deep sea animals ◄ Poisonous animals ◄
Sea animals ◄ Seashore animals ◄

Starfish are round or circular. They are part of the group of animals called echinoderms. This group includes the ball-shaped spiny sea urchins, sausage-shaped crawling sea cucumbers, flower-like sea lilies and feather stars, which are attached by stalks to the ocean bottom. All 6,000 kinds of echinoderms live in the sea.

▶ Spiny ball

Like starfish, sea urchins have long, wavy, tube-shaped 'feet'. These poke out between their long spines, which can tilt at their bases. A starfish 'walks' on its feet and spines and uses its five-part mouth to scrape tiny animals and plants from rocks.

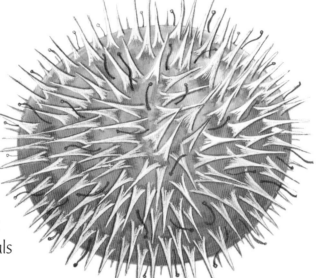

▲ Common starfish

The starfish is a predator. When it finds a shellfish to eat, the starfish slowly pulls the shell open — then turns its own stomach inside out, through its mouth on the underside, to eat the soft insides.

Wow!
If a sea cucumber is in danger from an enemy, it throws its guts out of its mouth!

◄ Pencil urchin

All echinoderms have a circular body shape, like a wheel with spokes. This is usually based on the number five. This means that most starfish have 5, 10 or 15 arms, and so on. Most urchins have a five-part body too, like an orange with five segments. Pencil urchins have spines that look like thick crayons. A few types of urchins have poison in their spines too.

Swamp animals

Find out more:
Cats ◀ Crocodiles and alligators ◀
Flamingos and waders ◀ Reptiles ◀ Snakes ◀

Frogs and dragonflies are well suited to swamps, bogs and marshes. A swamp can almost dry out, then flood. So animals must be very adaptable, like lungfish who breathe air, deer who hide in thick reeds, snakes who dive for food and turtles who stay underwater for hours.

◀ Swamp croc

Caimans are types of crocodiles found in the Americas. They grow to 6 metres long and eat fish, lizards, snakes, turtles and sometimes mammals.

▼ Swamp cat

Of the big cats, the jaguar of Central and South America is most at home in water. It wades, swims and dives in the Amazon River to catch fish and turtles. It also eats snakes and tapirs.

▼ Swamp snake

The anaconda of South America is a type of boa-constrictor. It usually squeezes, or squashes, its prey to death.

▼ Swamp bird

The small night heron has a white plume behind each 'ear', which it raises to attract a mate. It stalks or wades quietly at night, hunting a range of smaller creatures.

Wow!

The anaconda is the world's bulkiest snake, weighing up to 250 kilograms — as much as four adult people.

Town and city animals

Find out more:
Birds ◀ Flies ◀ Mice and rats ◀
Pests ◀

We crowd together in cities. We cause noise and stress, and produce huge amounts of waste. Various animals share this habitat with us, too. They eat our leftover foods, nest in our buildings and enjoy our central-heating. Mammals such as rats, mice and foxes, birds like sparrows, starlings and pigeons, and insects such as flies, silverfish and cockroaches share towns and cities with people worldwide.

Word box

roost
a resting or sleeping place, usually for flying animals like birds, bats and insects

waste
rubbish that nobody wants

▼ City-dweller

The red fox is about at night, when there is less traffic and human activity. It learns routines quickly and visits rubbish tips, litter bins and garden heaps to sniff for any kind of food. It lives in a burrow called an earth, in a bank or under an outbuilding.

▶ Rats

Huge numbers of rats are found all over the world in towns and cities. They will eat almost anything and breed very quickly. Rats can cause diseases that are harmful to people.

▼ Town birds

The starling lives in flocks, which fly out of town by day to feed. They return at dusk (early evening) to roost on roofs. As with pigeons, their droppings cause damage to buildings. Starlings and pigeons can also spread disease.

▼ Sorting the rubbish

In North America the common raccoon is a regular visitor to rubbish bins and bags. It climbs well over fences and rooftops, and sorts out edible bits using its front paws.

raccoon

fox

rat

Tropical forest animals

Find out more:
Apes ◄ Bats ◄ Birds ◄
Butterflies and moths ◄ Insects ◄

Word box

canopy
the 'roof' of a forest, formed where tree branches, twigs and leaves form a continuous layer

timber
pieces of wood cut from trees

spider monkey

Tropical rainforests have the richest wildlife on Earth. There are members of every kind of animal group, from worms and grubs to elephants, crocodiles and gorillas. They also face great threats, as people cut down trees to sell for timber, then clear the ground for farmland.

▶ Insects

Millions of kinds of insect teem in tropical rainforests. This morpho butterfly of South America glitters blue to attract a mate and warn off predators as it flutters through the rainforest.

▼ On the ground

At ground level, the tropical rainforest can be quiet, dim and still. In South America, piglike peccaries snuffle for roots, shoots and grubs. One of their treats is fruit, dropped by birds and monkeys from high above.

▲ Tree mammals

Tree mammals include squirrels, tree rats and small types of wild cats. There are also monkeys such as the spider monkey of South America, which can grasp equally well with its hands, feet and tail.

◄ Birds

Most tropical rainforest life is 30 metres or more above the ground in its canopy of branches. In Africa and Asia, hornbills, such as this yellow hornbill, flap and squawk as they delicately pick small berries and fruits with their huge bills. Other rainforest birds include parrots, colourful sun-birds and birds of paradise.

Turtles and tortoises

Few animals are slower or safer than turtles, terrapins and tortoises. They form a group of reptiles called chelonians, with almost 300 types. Turtles and terrapins swim in water and have broad, flipper-shaped legs, while tortoises dwell mainly on land. All have a double-layered shell of bony plates covered with horny plates.

Wow!

The largest turtle is the leather-back of the ocean, which has a head and body almost 2 metres long. It measures nearly 3 metres across its front flippers.

Make a turtle shell

1. Put some papier mâché over a balloon, leaving holes for the turtle's head, tail and four legs.

2. When dry, paint the shell and then pop the balloon. Stick on four cardboard legs.

3. Put your arm through the tail hole and out through the head hole, making your fist into the turtle's head – draw eyes and a mouth on your fist!

▲ Giant tortoise

The biggest tortoises live on the Galapagos Islands in the Pacific Ocean. They grow to 1.2 metres long and weigh over 200 kilograms. Giant tortoises can live for more than 100 years.

▼ Slow and steady

The alligator snapping turtle of North America lies still in muddy water, with weeds growing on its shell. In its mouth it has a piece of wormlike flesh that it uses for bait. Fish come to look at the 'worm', and snap, the prey is caught!

alligator snapping turtle

◄ Race to the sea

Baby turtles hatch from eggs laid on a beach. They race to the sea, risking being snapped up on the way by gulls or crabs. Sadly, few young turtles reach adult life.

▼

Whales

The blue whale is the largest mammal.
There are about 40 different types of whales.
They spend hours underwater, coming
up only to breathe. They spout out
water from a blow-hole on top.

▼ Whale with a sword

The narwhal has an amazing
tusk —a very long upper left
tooth. Usually only males
grow the tusk. They 'fence'
with rivals at breeding time,
as if sword-fighting.

▲ Noisy whales

Belugas are probably the noisiest
whales. They chirp, chatter, wail
and moan to each other as they
swim along the coasts of the Arcti
Ocean. Many other whales also
send out squeaks and clicks and
listen to the bounced-back echoes
to detect objects around them.

▼ Sperm whale

Sperm whales can dive more than
1,000 metres into water and stay
beneath for more than an hour.

▼ Blue whale

The blue whale opens its mouth wide to gulp in water. It then squeezes the
water out through rows of bristly, strap-shaped plates called baleen. Small
animals called krill are trapped by the baleen and get eaten.

krill

baleen

Wolves and dogs

Wolves, wild dogs, foxes and jackals form a group known as **canids**. Most are predators but they can also survive on fruits, berries and scraps. Wolves and wild dogs form groups called packs. Foxes and jackals usually live as female and male parents with their young.

Word scramble

Unscramble these words to find the names of five types of canid:

a. DILW OGD
b. KLACAJ
c. OXF
d. GINOD
e. REYG FLOW

answers
a. wild dog b. jackal c. fox d. dingo e. grey wolf

► No escape

Once African wild (hunting) dogs start to chase a victim, there is little escape. They speed along at 40 kilometres an hour, bringing back meat for females with cubs, and for sick or injured pack members.

▲ Small cub, big ears

The African bat-eared fox is one of the smallest foxes. It uses its huge ears to detect insects. The cubs (young) like this one grow up with their parents and then leave to set up a family in their own area.

► Leader of the pack

Grey wolves live in packs of about ten members in most northern lands. Only one pair breed – the rest help by bringing food such as smaller mammals for the cubs in their den (home).

► Maned wolf

The maned wolf lives in South American grasslands. In some areas it is kept as a tame pet, but in other places it is killed as a night-time attacker of farm animals.

Woodland animals

Some woods go brown in winter, others stay green.
In deciduous woodlands the trees lose their leaves in autumn,
while in conifer woods they remain on the trees. These two main
kinds of woods have different types of animals. Most obvious
are birds and active mammals such as deer, wild pigs and
squirrels. Less familiar are hosts of smaller mice, voles,
lizards, snakes, insects, spiders and worms.

green woodpecker

▲ Badger sett

Badgers and their young live in
tunnels and chambers called a sett,
lined with soft materials. At dusk
badgers look for mice, eggs, bugs,
grubs, berries, fruits and shoots.

► Woodpeckers

Woodpeckers peck wood to find their
favourite food of grubs and insects
under the bark. At breeding time they
chip at the wood to hollow out a hole
for a nest. The noise they make
hammering at the wood tells other
woodpeckers to stay away!

▼ Kiwi

Shy and secret, kiwis live in thick woodlands in New
Zealand. At night they feed on worms, grubs and
beetles, soft berries and fruits. If a predator
appears they cannot fly away – their
wings are too small.

▲ Wild boar

This wild pig (boar) is widespread
in woods across Europe, Asia and
Southeast Asia. Wild boar dig into
the ground with their snouts for
roots, bulbs, nuts, fruits and small
soil animals. Male wild boar live
close to herds of females. At
breeding time they fight rival
males with their tusks.

Worms

Worms are vital for the natural world. As earthworms tunnel through soil, eating bits of old plants, they let in air and moisture, so that new plants can grow. Worms in the sea eat the remains of dying animals, helping to recycle nutrients (goodness). A world without worms would quickly fill up with dead, rotting bodies!

▼ Inside a worm

An earthworm is a segmented worm or annelid. It has a head at one end, a tail at the other, and many segments in-between. Each segment contains the same set of organs.

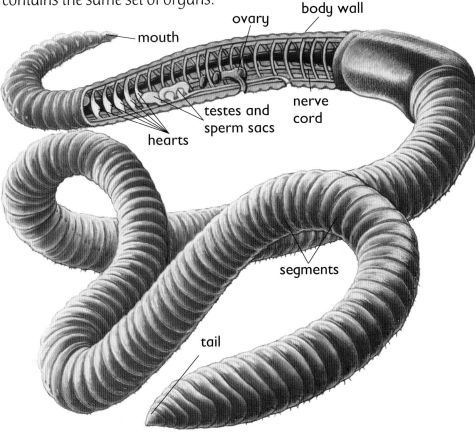

mouth

ovary

body wall

testes and sperm sacs

nerve cord

hearts

segments

tail

Make a wormery

1. Ask an adult to help you. In a see-through container, put a 5-centimetre layer of sand, then a 5-centimetre layer of soil, and then alternate the sand and soil until your container is almost full.
2. Add leaves to the very top
3. Take a few worms from your garden, add these to the container, and keep it in a cool, dark place.
4. Every few days, see how the worms mix up the layers.

▲ Roundworm

Roundworms are mostly tiny and simple. They live almost everywhere including soil, ponds, rivers, seas and inside plants and creatures. Some, such as hookworms and pinworms, cause diseases.

Wow!
The giant earthworms of southern Africa and southern Australia are thicker than your thumb and over 3 metres long!

▶ Fanworm

The head end of the fanworm has beautiful feathery tentacles that catch tiny pieces of food floating in the water. If danger appears, the worm whisks its 'fan' down into its burrow in the mud.

Index

The numbers in **bold** type refer to main entries in your book

**The publishers would like to thank
the following artists who have contributed
to this book:**
Syd Brak, John Butler, Martin Camm, Jim Channel,
Mark Davis, Richard Draper, Wayne Ford, Chris Forsey,
Terry Gabbey, Alan Harris, Ian Jackson, Stuart Lafford,
Doreen Mcguiness, Kevin Maddison, Maltings,
Janos Marffy, Andrea Morandi, Jonathan Pointer,
Steve Roberts, Eric Robson, Desiderio Sanzi,
Sarah Smith, Rudi Vizi, Steve Weston

**The publishers would like to thank Ted Smart
for the generous loan of his illustrations**

Photographic images:
Corel, digitalvision, PhotoDisc

All other pictures from the Miles Kelly Archives